KENT

A GENEALOGICAL BIBLIOGRAPHY

Volume 1

Genealogical Sources

by

Stuart A. Raymond

Published by the
Federation of Family History Societies (Publications) Ltd.,
The Benson Room, Birmingham & Midlands Institute,
Margaret Street, Birmingham, B3 3BS, U.K.

First published 1998

ISBN: 1-86006-071-4

ISSN: 1033-2065

Printed and bound by Oxuniprint, Great Clarendon Street, Oxford OX2 6DP

Contents

Introduction

This bibliography is intended primarily for genealogists. It is, however, hoped that it will also prove useful to historians, librarians, archivists, research students, and anyone else interested in the history of Kent. It is intended to be used in conjunction with my *English genealogy: an introductory bibliography,* and the other volumes in the *British genealogical bibliographies* series. A full list of these volumes appears on the back cover.

This volume lists works on a wide range of subjects of interest to Kent genealogists. Parish registers, monumental inscriptions, and probate records are listed in vol. 2; pedigrees, family histories, etc., are listed in vol.3. The whole work is exclusively concerned with published works, and numerous books and journal articles are listed. Numerous microfiche publications are also listed; Kent genealogists are fortunate in that the Kent Family History Society has issued well over 1800 microfiche publications, many of which reproduce original documents; most are listed here. However, the innumerable notes and queries to be found in family history society journals etc., are excluded, except where their content is of importance. Where I have included such notes, replies to them are cited in the form 'see also', with no reference to the names of respondents. I have also excluded extracts from newspapers, and histories which have not been published. Where possible, citations are accompanied by notes indicating the period covered, the locality/ies in which the families concerned dwelt, and other pertinent information. I have physically examined almost every item listed here, with the exception of a number of the Kent Family History Society's microfiche publications which are not to be found in any of the libraries I have used. These are noted 'not seen', as I have not been able to check their correct titles or contents.

Be warned: just because information has been published, it does not necessarily follow that it is accurate. I have not made any judgement on the accuracy of most works listed: that is up to you.

Anyone who tries to compile a totally comprehensive bibliography of Kent is likely to fall short of his aim. The task is almost impossible, especially if the endeavour is made by one person. That does not, however, mean that the attempt should not be made. Usefulness, rather than comprehensiveness, has

4

been my prime aim — and this book would not be useful to anyone if its publication were to be prevented by a vain attempt to ensure total comprehensiveness. I am well aware that there are likely to be omissions, especially in view of the fact that, given constraints of time and money, it has not been possible for me to visit all of the large number of libraries with substantial collections on Kent's history. Each of them may well possess works not held anywhere else. The identification of such works is not, however, a major aim of this bibliography. Rather, my purpose has been to enable you to identify works which are mostly readily available, and which can be borrowed via the inter-library loan network irrespective of whether you live in London or Melbourne. Most public libraries are able to tap into this network; your local library should be able to borrow most items I have listed, even if it has to go overseas to obtain them. The prominent exception to this rule are the microfiche publications of the Kent Family History Society, which ought to be in far more libraries than they actually are. No library has a complete set of these fiche, despite their importance. However, they are cheap and easily purchased.

If you are an assiduous researcher, you may well come across items I have missed. If you do, please let me know, so that they can be included in the next edition.

The work of compiling this bibliography has depended heavily on the resources of the libraries I have used. These included the Centre for Kentish Studies and Maidstone Reference Library at Maidstone, Canterbury Public Library, the Institute of Heraldic and Genealogical Studies, Canterbury Cathedral Archives, and the University of Kent library at Canterbury, the British Library, the Society of Genealogists, Guildhall Library, the Greater London Record Office, and Lewisham Local History Centre in London, the Central Library in Bristol, the University of Exeter library and the Exeter Public Library in Exeter. All these institutions deserve my thanks, as do Gillian Rickard and Brian Christmas, who have both read and commented on early drafts of the book. Mionie Dryden and Mark Gant typed the manuscript, and Bob Boyd saw the book through the press. I am grateful too to the officers of the Federation of Family History Societies, whose support is vital for the continuation of this series. My thanks also to my wife Marjorie, and to Paul and Mary, who have lived with this book for many months.

Stuart A. Raymond

Abbreviations

A.C.	*Archaeologia Cantiana.*
B.K.	*Bygone Kent.*
F.F.H.S.J.	*Folkestone Family History Society journal.*
F.H.S.	Family history society
J.K.L.H.	*Journal of Kent [local] history.*
K.C.	*The Kentish connection.*
K.F.H.S.J.	*Kent Family History Society journal.*
K.F.H.S.R.P.	Kent Family History Society record publications
M.G.H.	*Miscellanea genealogica et heraldica.*
N.S.	New series
N.W.K.F.H.	*North West Kent family history.*
T.G.L.A.S.	*Transactions of the Greenwich & Lewisham Antiquarian Society.*
W.D.A.S.A.R.	Woolwich District Antiquarian Society annual report.
W.D.F.H.S.J.	*Woolwich & District Family History Society journal.*

Bibliographic Presentation

Authors names are in SMALL CAPITALS. Book and journal titles are in *italics*. Articles appearing in journals, and material such as parish register transcripts, forming only part of books are in inverted commas and textface type. Volume numbers are in **bold** and the individual number of the journal may be shown in parentheses. These are normally followed by the place of publication (except where this is London, which is omitted), the name of the publisher and the date of publication. In the case of articles, further figures indicate page numbers.

Libraries and Record Offices

There are many libraries and record offices holding substantial collection relating to Kent genealogy; they cannot all be listed here. Various directories of libraries and archives are listed in Raymond's *English genealogy: bibliography,* and these should be consulted. The major repositories are:

Centre for Kentish Studies,
County Hall,
MAIDSTONE,
Kent,
ME14 1XQ

Canterbury Cathedral Archives,
The Precincts,
CANTERBURY,
Kent,
CT1 2EH

Rochester upon Medway Studies Centre,
Clock Tower Building,
Civic Centre,
STROOD,
Kent, ME2 4EW

THE HISTORY OF KENT

he purpose of genealogy is to trace our
ιcestral descent, and to place our forebears
ιthin the historical context in which they
ved. These aims cannot be achieved without
ι appreciation of the historical background.
enealogists ought to read the standard
.stories of the county or counties in which
ιeir ancestors lived, and to be aware of the
ιrious ways in which the sources used for
ɛnealogical research may also be used to
construct the world of the past. For Kent,
vast range of historical literature is
ɪailable, and only a very summary listing
ιn be given here. For further information,
ɪnsult the bibliographies listed in section 3
ɛlow.

he antiquarian county histories of the
ιneteenth century and earlier are often of
ιuch more immediate use to genealogists
ιan more recent studies, since they
ɛquently contain pedigrees and extracts
ɒm original records. A number of
ιtiquaries wrote parochial surveys of the
ɔunty; these include brief histories of each
arish, and frequently record manorial
ɛscents, monumental inscriptions, deed
ϰtracts, *etc.,* they are particularly useful for
ɛnealogists. The following listing is
ɪranged roughly by date of compilation.

ιAMDEN, WILLIAM. *Camden's Britannia, from
the edition of 1789 by Richard Gough,* ed.
Gordon J. Copley. Hutchinson, 1977.
ιAMBARDE, WILLIAM. *A perambulation of
Kent, conteining the description, hystorie
and customes of that shire, written in the
yeere 1570.* Baldwin, Cradock and Joy,
1826. Reprinted Bath: Adams & Dart, 1970,
with an introduction by Richard Church.
ιLBURNE, RICHARD. *A topographie, or,
survey, of the County of Kent, with some
chronological, historicall, and other
matters touching the same, and the
several parishes and places therein.* Henry
Atkinson, 1659.
ιCHOLS, JOHN. *Antiquities in Kent and
Sussex.* Biblioteca topographica
Britannica 1. J. Nichols, 1790. Parochial
survey, given lists of incumbents, many
inscriptions, extracts from deeds, *etc.*

HASTED, EDWARD. *The history and
topographical survey of the County of
Kent ...* 2nd ed. 12 vols. Canterbury: W.
Bristow, 1797-1801. Reprinted with a new
introduction by Alan Everitt, East Ardsley:
EP Publishing, 1972. Extensive parochial
survey; including many descents, lists of
clergy, monumental inscriptions, etc., etc.
Indexed in: *Edward Hasted: the history
and topographical survey of the County
of Kent: an index to parishes, hundreds
and lathes.* [ ]: Kent County Library, 1972.
FINCH, W. *An historical sketch of the
County of Kent, collected from the
celebrated works of Camden, Harris,
Seymour, Phillipot, Hastead, with a
directory ...* 2 pts. Daniel, 1803. Includes
brief histories of each parish, as well as a
concise directory of the gentry and
leading tradesmen.
IRELAND, W.H. *England's topographer, or, a
new and complete history of Kent, from
the earliest records to the present time ...*
4 vols. Geo. Virtue, 1828-30. Parochial
survey, including many descents.
GREENWOOD, C. *An epitome of county
history ... vol.l: Kent.* The author, 1838.
Parochial survey, including descents,
monumental inscriptions, *etc.*
Four similar works covering particular
regions of the county are:
FURLEY, ROBERT. *A history of the Weald of
Kent with an outline of the history of the
county to the present time.* 2 vols. in 3.
Ashford: Igglesden, 1871-4. Includes many
extracts from original sources.
HUGHSON, DAVID. *London: being an accurate
history and description of the British
metropolis and its neighbourhood to
thirty miles extent, from an actual
perambulation, vol. V.* J. Stratford, 1808.
Parochial survey; this volume covers
metropolitan parishes in Kent and
Surrey.
LYSONS, DANIEL. *The environs of London,
being an historical account of the towns,
villages and hamlets wiwhin twelve miles
of that capital, interspersed with
biographical anecdotes.* 2nd ed. T. Cadell
& W. Daves, 1811. Vol.l, pt. 1, provides a
parochial survey of Kent parishes on the
edge of London.

SMETHAM, HENRY. *Rambles around churches.* 4 vols. Chatham: Parret & Neves, 1925-9. Effectively a parochial survey of the Medway area.

For the buildings of Kent, see:

NEWMAN, JOHN. *North East and East Kent.* Buildings of England. 3rd ed. Harmondsworth: Penguin Books, 1983.

NEWMAN, JOHN. *West Kent and the Weald.* Buildings of England. 2nd ed. Harmondsworth: Penguin Books, 1976.

Biographies are not, in general, listed in this bibliography. However, there are two which are worth reading by all Kent genealogists:

WARNICKE, RETHA M. *William Lambarde: Elizabethan antiquary.* Phillimore, 1993. Includes bibliography.

JESSUP, FRANK W. *Sir Roger Twysden, 1597-1672.* Cresset Press, 1965. Includes useful list of 'manuscript material used'.

Modern historians do not provide the source materials printed by their antiquarian predecessors; they must, however, be read if you want to appreciate how your ancestors lived. A number of general works on Kent history have been published in recent years.

BRANDON, PETER, & SHORT, BRIAN. *The South East from A.D. 1000.* A regional history of England series. Longman, 1990. Covers Kent, Surrey and Sussex.

BUSHELL, T.A. *Kent.* The Barracuda guide to county history series 1. Chesham: Barracuda Books, 1976. A chronology

DETSICAS, ALEC, & YATES, NIGEL, eds. *Studies in modern Kentish history presented to Felix Hull and Elizabeth Melling on the occasion of the fiftieth anniversary of the Kent Archives Office.* Maidstone: Kent Archaeological Society, 1983.

JESSUP, FRANK W. *A history of Kent.* Darwen county history series. Rev. ed. Phillimore & Co., 1995.

EVERITT, ALAN. *Continuity and colonization: the evolution of Kentish settlement.* Leicester: Leicester University Press, 1986.

EVERITT, A.M. "The making of the agrarian landscape of Kent', *A.C.* **92**, 1976, 1-31.

HULL, FELIX. *Kent.* Ordnance Survey historical guides. George Philip/Ordnance Survey, 1988.

ROAKE, MARGARET, & WHYMAN, JOHN. *Essays in Kentish history.* Frank Cass, 1973. Reprints articles from *Archaeologia Cantiana.*

Many extracts from a wide variety of sources have been printed in Elizabeth Melling's *Kentish sources* series. These provide useful background information, and may contain the clue you are looking for. Relevant volumes are:

MELLING, ELIZABETH, ed. *Kentish sources, II: Kent and the civil war; a collection of examples from original sources in the Kent Archives Offices, illustrating opinions and events in the mid-seventeenth century.* Maidstone: Kent County Council, 1960.

MELLING, ELIZABETH, ed. *Kentish sources, III: aspects of agriculture and industry; a collection of examples from original sources in the Kent Archives Office, from the sixteenth to the nineteenth century.* Maidstone: Kent County Council, 1961. Includes 9 probate inventories, extracts from estate records, notes on the Best family of Chatham, *etc.*

MELLING, ELIZABETH, ed. *Kentish sources, IV: the poor; a collection of examples from original sources in the Kent Archives Office, from the sixteenth to the nineteenth century.* Maidstone: Kent County Council, 1964.

MELLING, ELIZABETH, ed. *Kentish sources, V: some Kentish houses: a collection of examples from original sources in the Kent Archives Office, from the fifteenth to the nineteenth century.* Maidstone: Kent County Council, 1965. Includes extracts from probate inventories, estate records, *etc.*

MELLING, ELIZABETH, ed. *Kentish sources, VI: crime and punishment; a collection of examples from original sources in the Kent Archives Office, from the sixteenth to the nineteenth century.* Maidstone: Kent County Council, 1969. Based on Quarter sessions records.

YATES, NIGEL, ed. *Kentish sources, VII: Kent and the Oxford Movement; selected documents.* Gloucester: Alan Sutton for Kent Archives Office, 1983. 19th c.

HYMAN, J. *Kentish sources, VIII: the early Kentish seaside (1736-1840): selected documents.* Gloucester: Alan Sutton, for Kent Archives Office, 1985

LOOMFIELD, PETER, ed. *Kentish sources, X: Kent and the Napoleonic wars; selected documents.* Gloucester: Alan Sutton for Kent Archives Office, 1987.

umerous works are available dealing with articular periods. A select few of these are sted here in rough chronological order

Medieval Period, to 1500

ITNEY, K.P. *The Jutish forest: a study of the Weald of Kent from 450 to 1380 A.D.* Athlone Press, 1976.

ITNEY, K.P. 'The woodland economy of Kent, 1066-1348', *Agricultural history review* **38**, 1990, 20-39.

ALES, R. 'Local loyalties in Norman England: Kent in Stephen's reign', *Anglo-Norman studies: proceedings of the Battle conference* **8**, 1986, 88-108.

U BOULAY, F.R.H. *The Lordship of Canterbury: an essay on medieval society.* Nelson, 1966. Social and economic history of the Archbishopric's estates; includes pedigree of Eynsford, 12-13th.

EBSTER, BRUCE. 'The community of Kent in the reign of Richard II', *A.C.* **100**, 1985, 217-29.

ROOKS, N. 'The organization and achievement of the peasants of Kent and Essex in 1381', *in* MAYR-HARTING, H., & MOORE, R.I., eds. *Studies in medieval history presented to R.H.C. Davis.* Hambleton Press, 1985, 247-70.

LEMING, P.W. 'Charity, faith, and the gentry of Kent, 1422-1509', *in* POLLARD, TONY, ed. *Property and politics: essays in later medieval history.* Gloucester: Alan Sutton, 1984, 36-58. Based on probate records.

U BOULAY, F.R.H. 'A rentier economy in the later middle ages', *Economic history review* 2nd series **16**, 1964, 427-38. General study of a major landed estate.

Early Modern Period, 1500-1700

LARK, PETER. *English provincial society from the Reformation to the Revolution: religion, politics and society in Kent, 1500-1640.* Hassocks, Kent: Harvester Press, 1977. Required reading.

CLARK, P. 'Reformation and radicalism in Kentish towns, c.1500-1553', in MOMMSEN, W.J., et al, eds. *Stadtbürgertum und Ald in der Reformation / The urban classes, the nobility and the Reformation.* Publications of the German Historical Institute, London **5**. Stuttgart: Klett/Cotta, 1979, 107-27.

JORDAN, W.K. *Social institution in Kent, 1480-1660: a study of the changing pattern of social aspirations.* Kent Archaeological Society, 1961. Published as *A.C.* **75**. Study of bequests to charities, based on an extensive analysis of wills

COCKBURN, J.S. 'Patterns of violence in English society: homicide in Kent, 1500-1985', *Past and present* **130**, 1991, 70-106. Based on assize records.

O'HARA, DIANA. 'The language of tokens and the making of marriage', *Rural history* **3**, 1992, 1-40. Based on depositions in Canterbury diocesan courts.

ZELL, MICHAEL. *Industry in the countryside: Wealden society in the sixteenth century.* Cambridge: Cambridge University Press, 1994.

ZELL, MICHAEL. 'Population and family structure in the sixteenth-century Weald', *A.C.* **100**, 1985, 231-57. Based on parish registers.

ZELL, MICHAEL. 'A wood-pasture agrarian regime: the Kentish Weald in the sixteenth century', *Southern history.* **7**, 1985, 69-93.

DAVIS, JOHN F. *Heresy and reformation in the South-East of England, 1520-1559.* Studies in history series **34**. Royal Historical Society, 1983. Based on records relating to the Weald, northern Essex, and London.

SCHULER, S. *Die Klostersakularisation in Kent, 1535-1558.* Paderborn: Ferdinand Schöningh, 1980. In German. Includes list of stewards, bailiffs, etc., of monastic lands at the dissolution.

O'HARA, DIANA. 'Ruled by my friends: aspects of marriage in the Diocese of Canterbury, c.1540-1570', *Continuity and change* **6**(1), 1991, 9-41.

ZELL, MICHAEL L. 'The mid-Tudor market in crown land in Kent', *A.C.* **97**, 1982, 53-70. Discussion of the dispersal of Crown property, especially that derived from ecclesiastical estates.

MOORE, JOHN S. 'Canterbury visitations and the demography of mid-Tudor Kent', *Southern history* **15**, 1993, 36-85.

LOADES, D.M. *Two Tudor conspiracies.* Cambridge; 1965 Includes discussion of Wyatt's rebellion.

CLARK, PETER. 'Popular protest and disturbance in Kent 1558-1640', *Economic history review* 2nd series **29**, 1976, 365-82.

CHALKLIN, C.W. *Seventeenth-century Kent.* Longmans, 1965. Important.

BOWER, JACQUELINE. 'The Kent yeoman in the seventeenth century', *A.C.* **114**, 1995, 149-63.

KNAFLA, LOVIS A. 'Sin of all sorts swarmeth: criminal litigation in an English county in the early seventeenth century', in IVES, E.W., & MANCHESTER, A.H., eds. *Law, litigants and the legal profession.* Studies in history **36**. Royal Historical Society, 1983, 50-67. Based on the records of various Kentish courts.

ARMSTRONG, ALAN, ed. *The economy of Kent, 1640-1914.* Kent history project. Woodbridge: Boydell Press, 1995.

YATES, NIGEL, & HUME, ROBERT, & HASTINGS, PAUL. *Religion and society in Kent, 1640-1914.* Kent history project. Woodbridge: Boydell Press, 1994. Collection of essays.

LASLETT, PETER. 'The gentry of Kent in 1640', *Cambridge historical journal* **9**(2), 1948, 148-64.

WOODS, T.P.S. *Prelude to civil war: Mr. Justice Malet and the Kentish petitions.* Salisbury: Michael Russell, 1980.

ABELL, HENRY FRANCIS. *Kent and the Great Civil War.* Ashford: Kentish Express, 1901.

EVERITT, ALAN. *The community of Kent and the Great Rebellion.* Leicester: Leicester University Press, 1973. Authoritative.

HUME, R. 'Educational provision for the Kentish poor, 1660-1811: fluctuations and trends', *Southern history* **4**, 1982, 123-44. General study.

BONFIELD, L. 'Marriage settlements, 1664-1740: the adoption of strict settlement in Kent and Northamptonshire', in OUTHWAITE, R.B., ed. *Marriage and society: studies in the social history of marriage.* Europa Publications, 1981, 101-16.

LEE, COLIN. 'Fanatic magistrates: religious and political conflict in three Kent boroughs, 1680-1684', *Historical journal* **35**, 1992, 43-61. The boroughs considered are Dover, Canterbury and Sandwich.

DOBSON, MARY J. 'The last hiccup of the old demographic machine: population stagnation and decline in late seventeenth and early eighteenth-century South-East England', *Continuity and change* **4**(3), 1989, 395-428. Demographic study of Kent, Essex and Sussex.

Eighteenth Century

GROVER, R. 'Early land tax assessments explored, 2: Kent and Sussex', in TURNER M., & MILLS, D., eds. *Land and property: the English land tax 1692-1832,* New York St. Martin Press, 1986, 204-18.

SOUDEN, DAVID, & LASKER, GABRIEL. 'Biological inter-relationships between parishes in East Kent: an analysis of Marriage & Duty Act returns for 1705', *Local population studies* **21**, 1978, 30-39.

LANDAU, NORMA. 'The laws of settlement and the surveillance of immigration in eighteenth-century Kent', *Continuity and change* **3**, 1988, 391-420. See also **6**(3), 1991, 375-439. This and the following two works debate the effect of the settlement laws on Kent, and illustrate how historians use genealogical sources for non-genealogical purposes.

SNELL, K.D.M. 'Pauper settlement and the right to poor relief in England and Wales the eighteenth-century context of the laws of settlement', *Continuity and change* **6**(3 1991, 375-439.

LANDAU, NORMA. 'The regulation of immigration: economic structures and definitions of the poor in eighteenth-century England', *Historical journal* **33**, 1990, 541-72.

Nineteenth & Twentieth Centuries

REAY, BARRY. *The last rising of the agricultural labourers: rural life and protest in nineteenth-century England.* Oxford: Clarendon Press, 1990. Background to the Battle of Bossenden Wood.

REAY, BARRY. 'The last rising of the agricultural labourers: the battle of Bossenden Wood, 1838', *History workshop* **26**, 1988, 79-101.

ARMSTRONG, W.A. 'The population of Victorian and Edwardian Kent', *A.C.* **112**, 1994, 1-16; **114**, 1995, 17-37. Based on the census, parish registers, *etc.*

CONLEY, CAROLYN A. *The unwritten law: criminal justice in Victorian Kent.* Oxford: Oxford University Press, 1991.

CROSSICK, GEOFFREY. *An artisan elite in Victorian society: Kentish London 1840-1880.* Croom Helm, 1978.

MELLING, ELIZABETH. *History of the Kent County Council, 1889-1974.* Maidstone: Kent County Council, 1975. Includes lists of councillors, officers, etc.

MOYLAN, PRUDENCE ANN. *The form and reform of county government: Kent 1889-1914.* Dept. of English Local History occasional papers **3**. Leicester: Leicester University Press, 1978.

ARMSTRONG, W.A. 'Kentish rural society during the first world war', in HOLDERNESS, B.A., & TURNER, MICHAEL E., eds. *Land, labour and agriculture 1700-1920: essays for Gordon Mingay.* Hambledon Press, 1991, 109-31.

2. PARISH AND LOCAL HISTORIES

Innumerable histories of particular places in Kent are available; a full listing is well beyond the scope of this book, and reference should be made to the bibliographies listed in section 3 below to identify other works. This listing attempts to identify those works which have a particular value to genealogists — works which either include substantial extracts from original sources, which use genealogical source material for wider historical study, or which have a wider importance than the merely local.

Ash
NEWMAN, A. 'An evaluation of bastardy recordings in an East Kent parish', in LASLETT, PETER,& OOSTERVEEN, KARLA, & SMITH, RICHARD M., eds. *Bastardy and its comparative history: studies in the history of illegitimacy and marital nonconformism in Britain, France, Germany, Sweden, North America, Jamaica, and Japan.* Arnold, 1980, 141-57. Based on the parish registers of Ash next Sandwich, 1654-1840.

Ashford
PEARMAN, A.J. *Ashford: its church, vicars, college and grammar school.* Ashford: Thompson, 1886. Includes list of vicars, many inscriptions, list of schoolmasters, *etc.*

RUDERMAN, ARTHUR. *A history of Ashford.* Chichester: Phillimore, 1994. Includes lists of manorial lords, clergy, grammar school masters, improvement commissioners, *etc.,* also various extracts from original sources.

See also Hythe

Barming
SCHOFIELD, ROGER. 'Traffic in corpses: some evidence from Barming, Kent, (1788-1812)', *Local population studies* **33**, 1984, 49-53. Argues that no less than 28% of burials in Barming were of persons who died elsewhere.

Benenden

HASLEWOOD, FRANCIS. *The parish of Benenden, Kent, its monuments, vicars and persons of note* ... Ipswich: the author, 1889. Includes many inscriptions, brief biographies of vicars, pedigree of Munn, 17-19th c., wills, *etc.*

Bexley

DU BOULAY, F.R.H. *Medieval Bexley.* Bexley: Bexley Corporation Public Libraries, 1961. Scholarly; includes list of sources.

Blackheath Hundred

DUNKIN, ALFRED JOHN. *History of the County of Kent: Hundred of Blackheath.* John Russell Smith, 1855. Includes many extracts from wills and other sources.

DRAKE,H.H. *Hasted's history of Kent: Hundred of Blackheath, corrected, enlarged, and continued to the present time ... Part 1: the Hundred of Blackheath.* Mitchell & Hughes, 1886. Microfiche edition (11 fiche). K.F.H.S.R.P. **1652.** 1992. Includes folded pedigrees of Evelyn and Drake.

Boughton

REAY, BARRY. 'Before the transition: fertility in English villages', *Local population studies* 9(1), 1994, 91-120. Based on the parish register of Boughton, Dunkirk, and Hernhill.

Boxley

CAVE-BROWN, J. *The history of Boxley parish: the Abbey, rood of grace, and abbots; the clergy; the church, monuments, and registers; including an account of the Wiat family, and of the trial on Penenden Heath in 1076.* Maidstone: E.J. Dickinson, 1892. Includes extensive extracts from the parish register, 1558-1808.

Brenchley

WOJCIECHOWSKA, B. 'Brenchley: a study of migratory movements in a mid-nineteenth century rural parish', *Local population studies* **41**, 1988, 28-40.

Bromley

CLINCH, GEORGE. *Antiquarian jottings relating to Bromley, Hayes, Keston, and West Wickham in Kent.* Edinburgh: Turnbull & Spears, 1889. Includes notes on inscriptions, the parish registers, rectors and vicars, etc.

HORSBURGH, E.R.S. *Bromley, Kent, from the earliest times to the present century.* Hodder and Stoughton, 1929. Reprinted with new introduction, East Ardsley: S.R. Publications, 1971. Extensive history; includes list of clergy and extracts from various sources *etc.*

MCDONNELL, K.G.T. *Medieval London suburbs.* Phillimore, 1978. One of the suburbs studied in detail is Bromley.

Canterbury

BUTCHER, A.F. 'Rent and the urban economy; Oxford and Canterbury in the later middle ages', *Southern history* **1**, 1979, 11-43.

SOMNER, WILLIAM. *The antiquities of Canterbury, or, a survey of that ancient city, with the suburbs and cathedral, containing principally matters of antiquity in them all, collected chiefly from old manuscripts, lieger-books, and other like records for the most part not before printed, with an appendix here annexed, wherein ... the muniments and records of chiefest consequence are faithfully exhibited.* 2nd ed. revised by Nicolas Battely. R. Knaplock, 1703. Reprinted in facsimile, with a new introduction by William Urry, East Ardsley: E.P. Publishing, 1977.

URRY, WILLIAM. *Canterbury under the Angevin kings.* Athlone Press, 1967. Includes extensive 12-13th c. rentals.

Chartham

LANGRIDGE, ANGELA M. 'The population of Chartham from 1086 to 1600', *A.C.* **101**, 1985, 217-44. Demographic study based on manorial records, wills, the parish register, *etc.*

Chatham

See Rochester

Chislehurst

WEBB, E.A.,& MILLER, G.W., & BECKWITH, J. *The history of Chislehurst, its church, manors and parish.* George Allen, 1899. Extensive; includes manorial descents, notes on, and extracts from the parish registers, wills, inscriptions, lists of clergy, *etc., etc.*

Chislet

HASLEWOOD, FRANCIS. *The parish of Chislet, Kent: its monuments, vicars and parish officers, with a digest of ancient documents now remaining in the parish chest.* Ipswich: the author, 1887. Includes many 'cess' lists *etc.*

Dartford

DUNKIN, J. *The history & antiquities of Dartford, with topographical notices of the neighbourhood.* John Russell Smith, 1844. Includes lists of clergy and inscriptions, with many extracts from records, *etc.*

ROOME, K.M. 'Dartford, 1660 to c.1720', *A.C.* **111**, 1993, 113-21. Includes list of tradesmen derived from the parish register, wills, *etc.*

Davington

WILLEMENT, THOMAS. *Historical sketch of the parish of Davington, in the County of Kent, and of the Priory there dedicated to S. Mary Magdalene ...* Basil Montagu Pickering, 1862. Includes rental of the Priory, 1543/4, manorial descent, 17-19th c., notes on the parish register, memorial inscriptions, *etc.*

Deptford

DEWS, NATHAN. *The history of Deptford, in the counties of Kent and Surrey, compiled from authentic records and manuscripts.* 2nd ed. Conway Maritime Press, 1971. Originally published 1884. Includes pedigrees of Evelyn, 18-19th c., Pett, 13-19th c., and much information on 'worthies and men of note'.

DUNKIN, ALFRED JOHN. *History of the County of Kent: Deptford.* John Russell Smith, 1854. 'Hundred of Blackheath', at head of title page. Re-published on 5 fiche, K.F.H.S.R.P. **44**. 1985.

Dover

JONES, J.B. *Annals of Dover, including histories of the castle, port, passage, religion, the corporation, mayors & their times, corporation officials, representation in Parliament and social history.* 2nd ed. Dover: Dover Express Works, 1938. Includes biographical information on mayors *etc.*

Dunkirk

REAY, BARRY. 'The context and meaning of popular literacy: some evidence from nineteenth-century rural England', *Past and present* **131**, 1991, 89-129. Based on evidence from Boughton under Blean, Hernhill and Dunkirk.

See also Boughton and Hernehill

East Peckham

LAWRENCE, MARGARET. *Through this door: St Michael's church, East Peckham, illustrated by the parish registers, 1558-1972, and other sources.* [East Peckham]: [The church?] [1972?] Brief parish history with many biographical notices.

Eastry

SHAW, WILLIAM FRANCIS. *Liber Estriae, or, memorials of the royal ville and parish of Eastry in the County of Kent.* John Russell Smith, 1870. Includes many inscriptions, lists of clergy, clerks, and sextons, notes on families, extracts from wills, terriers of 1598, 1637 and 1833, *etc.*

East Wickham

See Plumstead

Farningham

BLACK, SHIRLEY BURGOYNE. *Local government, law and order in a pre-Reform English parish, 1790-1834.* Lewiston: Mellen University Press, 1992. Scholarly study of Farningham.

Faversham

JACOB, EDWARD. *History of Faversham.* Sheerness: Arthur J. Cassell for the Faversham Society, 1974. Originally published 1774. Includes list of mayors, 13-18th c., notes on benefactors, list of interments, *etc.*

Goudhurst

TIFFIN, ALFRED W. *The Goudhurst jubilee book: a record of celebrations in Goudhurst and Kilndown (Kent) on May 6th 1935, the silver jubilee of the reign of their Majesties King George V and Queen Mary, 1914-1935: local intelligence, directories, historical notes and reminiscences.* Tunbridge Wells: Courier Printing & Publishing Co., 1935. Includes 'directory of householders', *etc.*

TIFFIN, ALFRED W. *The Goudhurst coronation book: a record of celebrations in Goudhurst and Kilndown (Kent) on May 12th 1937, the coronation of their Majesties King George VI and Queen Elizabeth: directory, reminiscences and local lore.* Tunbridge Wells: Courier Printing & Publishing Co., 1937. Includes a 'directory of householders', *etc.*

Hartlip

PERKYNS, AUDREY. 'Birthplace accuracy in the censuses of six Kentish parishes 1851-81', *Local population studies* **47**, 1891, 39-55. The parishes concerned are Hartlip, Newington, Rainham, Stockbury, Upchurch and Lower Halstow.

Hayes

See Bromley

Herne

BUCHANAN, JAMES ROBERT. *Memorials of Herne.* 4th ed. Elliot Stock, 1887. Includes wills, notes on parish register, extracts from churchwardens' accounts, *etc.*

Hernhill

REAY, BARRY. 'Sexuality in nineteenth-century England: the social context of illegitimacy in rural Kent', *Rural history* **1**, 1990, 219-47. Based on the parish registers of Hernhill, Dunkirk, and Boughton under Blean.
See also Boughton under Blean

Hollingbourne

CAVE-BROWNE, J. *The story of Hollingborne, its church and its clergy.* Maidstone: E.J. Dickinson for the author, 1890. Includes extracts from the parish register, 1556-1800, notes on the clergy, monumental inscription, folded pedigrees of Colepepper and Cheyney, medieval-17th c., *etc.*

Hoo

HAMMOND, F.J. *The story of an outpost parish: Allhallows, Hoo, Kent.* S.P.C.K., [1928?] Includes chapters on the churchwardens' accounts, the overseers' book, and the parish register.

Hythe

DULLEY, A.J.F. 'Four Kent towns at the end of the middle ages', *A.C.* **81**, 1967, 95-108. Based on Arthor Hussey's abstracts of wills from Hythe, Milton, Ashford, and Sittingbourne.

Isle of Thanet

LEWIS, JOHN. *The history and antiquities as well ecclesiastical as civil, of the Isle of Tenet, in Kent.* 2nd ed. J. Osborn, 1736. Republished on 7 fiche, K.F.H.S.R.P. **156**. 1985.

Keston

See Bromley

Lower Halstow

See Rainham

Maidstone

CLARK, PETER, & MURFIN, LYN. *The history of Maidstone: the making of a modern county town.* Stroud: Alan Sutton, 1995.

RUSSELL, J.M. *The history of Maidstone.* Rochester: John Hallewell Publications, 1978. Facsimile; originally published 1881. Antiquarian study; includes chapter on 'old houses and families'.

Margate

WHYMAN, JOHN. 'A Hanoverian watering-place. Margate before the railways', in EVERITT, ALAN, ed. *Perspectives in English urban history.* Macmillan, 1973, 138-60. General study.

WHYMAN, JOHN. 'Visitors to Margate in the 1841 census returns: an attempt to look at the age and social structure of Victorian holidaymaking', *Local population studies* **8**, 1972, 19-38. Includes extracts of 1851 census for Bridge Street and Buenos Aires.

Meopham

GOLDING-BIRD, C.H. *The history of Meopham: a Kentish village from Saxon times.* Williams and Norgate, 1934. Includes list of burials in the churchyard, much information on the clergy, list of churchwardens, various extracts from original sources, *etc.*

Mersham

MILLS, JENNY. *Mersham during the eighteenth and early nineteenth centuries, including a survey of inhabitants by Edward Finn, (1794-1873).* Mersham: [ ], 1995.

Milton next Sittingbourne

See Hythe

Newington

See Hartlip

Otterden

FILMER, BRUCE J. 'Persons associated with medieval Otterden', *K.F.H.S.J.* **6**(9), 1991, 306-7. Includes list of surnames.

Plumstead

ELLISTON-ERWOOD, F.C., & MANDY, WILLIAM H. *The history of the church, manor and parish of Plumstead, with East Wickham in Kent in the middle ages.* 2 vols. New records of the Woolwich District **1**. Ascham Press for the Woolwich and District Antiquarian Society, 1937.

Rainham

PERKYNS, AUDREY. 'Age checkability and accuracy in the censuses of six Kentish parishes, 1851-1881', *Local population studies* **50**, 1993, 19-38. The parishes concerned are Rainham, Stockbury, Hartlip, Newington, Upchurch and Lower Halstow.

PERKYNS, AUDREY. 'Middle class yeomanry in the Kentish parish of Rainham in the nineteenth century', *Local historian* **26**(1), 1996, 16-35. General study; includes 18-19th c. pedigrees of Dodd, Gilbert, Mansfield, Miles, Smart and Wakeley.

See also Hartlip

Rochester

DULLEY, A.J.F. 'People and homes in the Medway towns, 1687-1783', *A.C.* **77**, 1963, 160-76. Analysis of probate inventories for Rochester, Chatham, Strood, and St. Margaret.

SMITH, FREDERICK FRANCIS. *A history of Rochester.* Rochester: John Hallewell Publications, 1976. Facsimile reprint; originally published 1923. Includes lists of mayors and M.Ps., also lists of councillors in 1629, 1923, and 1927, and extracts from original sources.

Romney Marsh

TEICHMAN-DERVILLE, M. *The level and the liberty of Romney Marsh in the County of Kent: an inquiry into the origin, history and present state of the two reputed corporations known as the lords, bailiffs and jurats of Romney Marsh, (the Level of Romney Marsh), and the bailiff jurats and commonalty of Romney Marsh (the Liberty of Romney Marsh), with some account of their ancient courts and early forms of land drainage administration.* Ashford: Headley Brothers, 1936. Includes descents of 23 manors, list of lords of Romney Marsh, roll of bailiffs, and detailed list of manuscript sources.

Saint Lawrence in Thanet

COTTON, CHARLES. *The history and antiquities of the church and parish of St. Laurence, Thanet, in the county of Kent.* Simpkin Marshall Hamilton, Kent & Co., 1895. Includes notes on 327 inscriptions, lists of clergy and churchwardens, folded pedigrees of Criollor, Kerioll, St. Nicholas, Johnson, Garrett, Sprakeling, and Curling, *etc., etc.* Extensive.

St. Margaret

See Rochester

Sandwich

BOYS, WILLIAM. *Collections for an history of Sandwich in Kent, with notices of the other Cinque Ports and members, and of Richborough.* Canterbury: Simmons, Kirkby and Jones, 1892. Includes list of monumental inscriptions, lists of M.Ps., mayors, stewards, bailiffs and town clerks, deed abstracts, *etc., etc.* Extensive.

Sevenoaks

LANSBERRY, H.C.F. 'Free bench see-saw: Sevenoaks widows in the late seventeenth century', *A.C.* **100**, 1985, 281-93. Discussion of testamentary provisions for widows.

Sittingbourne
See Hythe

Smarden

HASLEWOOD, FRANCIS. *Memorials of Smarden, Kent.* Ipswich: the author, 1886. Includes brief biographies of rectors, monumental inscriptions, extracts from parish records, wills, *etc.*

Staplehurst

ZELL, MICHAEL. 'Families and households in Staplehurst, 1563-64', *Local population studies* **33**, 1984, 54-7. Based on a household enumeration.

ZELL, M.L. 'The social parameters of probate records in the sixteenth century', *Bulletin of the Institute of Historical Research* **57**, 1984, 107-13. Analysis of the social standing of testators in Staplehurst, late 16th c.

Stockbury
See Hartlip

Strood

SMETHAM, HENRY. *History of Strood.* Rochester: John Hallewell, 1978. Facsimile. Originally published 1899.
See also Rochester

Upchurch
See Hartlip

Walmer

ELVIN, CHARLES R.S. *Records of Walmer ...* Henry Gray, 1890. Includes descent of the manor, with pedigrees of D'Auberville, 12-13th c., De Criol, 12-15th c., and Fogge, 15-18th c., notes on incumbents, monumental inscriptions, 18 brief biographies of local worthies (with pedigree of Boys, 18-19th c.) *etc., etc.* Extensive.

West Malling

LAWSON, A.W. *A history of the parish church of St. Mary the Virgin, West Malling, Kent.* West Malling, Kent: Henry C.H. Oliver, 1904. Includes monumental inscriptions, lists of vicars and churchwardens, list of parish records with some extracts, *etc.*

West Farleigh

'The Hannen papers', *A.C.* **46**, 1934, 215-6. Brief list of an antiquary's collection, including much material relating to West Farleigh.

West Wickham

KNOWLDEN, PATRICIA. 'Inhabitants of West Wickham before 1700', *K.C.* 3(4), 1983, 132-3. List derived from the author's researches.

KNOWLDEN, PATRICIA E. 'West Wickham and North-West Kent in the Civil War', *Local historian* **22**, 1992, 138-43. Includes useful references to source material.
See also Bromley

Westerham

LEVESON-GOWER, GRANVILLE. *Parochial history of Westerham.* Mitchell and Hughes, 1883. Includes numerous extracts from the parish registers, 16-19th c., etc.

Woolwich

VINCENT, W.T. *The records of the Woolwich district.* Woolwich: J.P. Jackson [188-?] Mentions innumerable names; includes notes on, and portraits of, 144 'local celebrities'. Extensive.

Wye

ORWIN, C.S. & WILLIAMS, S. *A history of Wye church and Wye College.* Ashford: Kentish Express, 1913. Includes biographical notes on clergy, extracts from parish registers, abstracts of ecclesiastical presentments, *etc.*

3. BIBLIOGRAPHY AND ARCHIVES.

A. General Bibliography

The literature on Kentish history is extensive; unfortunately, no one library holds a comprehensive collection — although the Centre for Kentish Studies at Maidstone has substantial holdings. Fortunately, the *Kent bibliography* provides a union listing of the holdings of the many local studies libraries in the historic county (including the holdings of London boroughs formerly in Kent). This is now out-dated, but still useful. See:
BENNETT, GEORGE. *The Kent bibliography: a finding list of Kent material in the public libraries of the county and of the adjoining London boroughs.* Library Association London and Home Counties Branch, 1977. Supplemented by:
BURGESS, WYN. *The Kent bibliography: a finding list of Kent material in the public libraries of the County and of the adjoining London boroughs ... Supplement.* Library Association London and Home Counties Branch, 1981.
A much older listing of Kentish works has been recently reprinted:
SMITH, JOHN RUSSELL. *Bibliotheca Cantiana: a bibliographical account of what has been published on the history, antiquities, customs, and family history of the County of Kent.* John Russell Smith, 1837. Reprinted as *Bibliotheca Cantiana, or, antiquarian Kentish books, volume 1, being an account of the published material, books, acts of Parliament, maps and ephemera, relating to the County of Kent up to the year 1836.* Chatham: John Hallewell Publications, 1980.
For town guides, see:
GOULDEN, R.J. *Kent town guides 1763-1900: a bibliography of locally published town guides, together with accounts of the printing, publishing and production of town guides in certain towns in Kent.* British Library, 1995.
Other general works include:
JESSUP, FRANK WILLIAM. *The history of Kent: a select bibliography.* 2nd ed. Maidstone: Kent Educational Committee, 1974. Brief.

KENT COUNTY LIBRARY. *Local history catalogue.* Maidstone: the Library, 1939.
Kent: a select list of references in periodical articles published during 1986. [Springfield]: Kent County Library, 1967. Continued annually or bi-annually until 1972.
Kent: a list of books about Kent added to the county library from 1974-1976. [Maidstone]: Kent County Council Education Committee, 1978.

B. Miscellaneous Libraries and Societies etc.

Kent Archaeological Society
The catalogue of this society's library on Kent's history and archaeology is printed in:
KELLY, D.B. 'Kent Archaeological Society library', *A.C.* **80**, 1966, 243-5; **81**, 1967, 219-34; **82**, 1968, 277-81; **83**, 1969, 277-80; **84**, 1970, 261-3; **85**, 1971, 215-21; **86**, 1971, 249.
See also:
'Descriptive catalogue of documents belonging to the Kent Archaeological Society', *A.C.* **25**, 1902, 256-98. Primarily a calendar of Oxenden family deeds, 14-18th c., and a transcript of the Isle of Sheppey ferry-wardens' accounts and orders, 16-17th c.

Kent Family History Society
Many manuscripts, published pedigrees and other genealogical books and papers in this society's library are listed in:
'Library report', *K.F.H.S.J.* passim.
The society has also undertaken an extensive programme of microfiching records of interest to genealogists, which other family history societies would do well to imitate. The material includes parish registers, monumental inscriptions, will abstracts, other parish records, *etc., etc.* Most of this material is listed at appropriate points in this bibliography; for a comprehensive listing, see:
List and index of Kent Family History Society's microfiche publications. Folkestone: Kent Family History Society, 1995. N.B. Many fiche have been added since this list was published; most are listed in the appropriate place below (or in the other volumes of this work). New fiche are regularly listed in *K.F.H.S.J.*

Lambeth Palace Library
The archives of the Archbishop of Canterbury are held at Lambeth Palace. A number of works briefly describe material relevant to Kent:

HORWOOD, ALFRED J. 'Lambeth Palace', in HISTORICAL MANUSCRIPTS COMMISSION. *Sixth report ...* pt. 1. C.1745. H.M.S.O., 97 1877, 522-4. Brief calendar, noting various Kentish documents.

KERSHAW, S.W. 'Lambeth Palace Library, and its Kentish memoranda', *A.C.* **9**, 1874, 176-88. Lists Kentish archival collections.

KERSHAW, S.W. 'Kent in the Lambeth archives', *Journal of the British Archaeological Association* **3**, 1897, 185-91.

KERSHAW, W.S. 'Kentish annals in Lambeth Library', *A.C.* **29**, 1911, 206-16.

OWEN, DOROTHY M. *A catalogue of Lambeth manuscripts 889 to 901 (carta antiqua et miscellanee).* Lambeth Palace Library, 1968. Includes much Kentish material.

OWEN, DOROTHY M. 'Canterbury archiepiscopal archives in Lambeth Palace Library', *Journal of the Society of Archivists* **2**, 1960-64, 140-47.

North West Kent Family History Society
'North West Kent Family History Society', *Family tree magazine* **4**(5), 1988, 8.

University of Kent
'University of Kent at Canterbury: list of theses', *J.K.L.H.* **25**, 1987, 13. Brief list of theses on Kentish subjects; regularly updated in subsequent issues.

Woolwich & District Family History Society
KEYMER, FAITH. 'Guest Society: the Woolwich & District Family History Society', *Family tree magazine* **8**(1), 1991, 17.

C. Local Bibliography and Archives
Bexley
REILLY, LEONARD. *Family history in Bexley: a guide to tracing your Bexley ancestors.* Bexley: Bexley Libraries and Museums, 1993.

'Bexley Library Service (Local Studies Section): genealogical information', *N.W.K.F.H.* **1**(4), 1979, 110-12. Brief note.

'Bexley Local Studies Library', *N.W.K.F.H.* **4**(1), 1986, 33.

Bromley
BURCH, BRIAN. *A bibliography of printed material relating to Bromley, Hayes, and Keston in the County of Kent.* Bromley: Bromley Public Library, 1964. Includes 668 entries.

Faversham
HYDE, PATRICIA. *Faversham and district bibliography: primary sources.* 6 vols. Faversham studies 1. Faversham: Faversham Society, 1993. Detailed listing of archives in various repositories. Important.

HYDE, PATRICIA. *Faversham and district bibliography: secondary sources.* Faversham studies 2. Faversham: Faversham Society, 1993.

HYDE, PATRICIA, & HARRINGTON, DUNCAN. *Faversham Hundred records, volume 1: being an index and catalogue of 5257 original documents deposited at the Public Record Office, Centre for Kentish Studies, Canterbury Cathedral Archives and Lambeth Palace Library.* 8 fiche. Lyminge: Harrington Research Services, 1994.

Folkestone
FOLKESTONE PUBLIC LIBRARY. *Some sources of information on places in Kent: a guide to the local collection contained in the reference library.* Folkestone: the library, 1931. Bibliography.

K.A.O. catalogues, S.E. Branch, Folkestone: unofficial documents. 3 fiche. K.F.H.S.R.P. **756**. 1986. Lists a wide range of documents held at Folkestone.

K.A.O. catalogues, S.E. Branch, Folkestone: F1982, F/NS, P87, 87A, 148, 148C, 148D, 148E, S/KR, HY, RD/El, RD/Ct, RD/Sg. 4 fiche. K.F.H.S.R.P. **757**. 1986. Catalogue of miscellaneous collections.

Greenwich
REILLY, LEONARD. *Family history in Greenwich: a guide to sources.* Greenwich Library, 1991. Brief list.

'Guide to family history resources at the Local History Library of the London Borough of Greenwich', *N.W.K.F.H.* **1**(2), 1979, 49-50. Brief note.

NUNN, F.W. 'A list of books, pamphlets, views, plans, etc., relating to Greenwich, with the press marks, as found in the reading room at the British Museum', *T.G.L.A.S.* 1(2), 1910, 75-100; 1(3), 1912, 155-8; 1(4), 1913, 223-43; 1(5), 1914, 313-28; 1(6) 1915, 397-411. Includes archival resources as well as books.

MONTMORENCY, J.E.G. DE. 'Greenwich records in the Record Office', *T.G.L.A.S.* 1(2), 1910, 67-74. i.e., the Public Record Office.

MONTMORENCY, J.E.G. DE. 'Greenwich manuscripts and maps in the British Museum', *T.G.L.A.S.* 1(2), 1910, 61-6.

REILLY, LEONARD. 'Books of local interest, 1983-1987', *T.G.L.A.S.* 10(3), 1987, 146-9.

WATSON, JULIAN. 'Recent books of local interest', 1(1), 1991, *Journal of the Greenwich Historical Society* 1(1), 1991, 42-4.

Catalogues: unofficial documents transferred to Greenwich. 1 fiche. K.F.H.S.R.P. 751. 1986.

Herne Bay

A list of books and references concerning Herne Bay, Herne and Reculver. [ ]: Kent County Library, 1951.

Isle of Thanet

GRITTEN, A.J. *Catalogue of books, pamphlets and excerpts dealing with Margate, the Isle of Thanet, and the county of Kent, in the local collection of the Borough of Margate Public Library.* Margate: Borough of Margate Public Library Committee, 1934.

Lewisham

HARRISON, CARL. 'Lewisham Archives and Local History Department', *N.W.K.F.H.* 1(2), 1979, 43-8. Includes list of major sources held.

VINCENT, W.T., et al, eds. 'Woolwich bibliography', *W.D.A.S.A.R.* 7-23, 1902-26, *passim.*

Sevenoaks

K.A.O. West Kent Area Office, Sevenoaks, unofficial documents ... 11 fiche. K.F.H.S.R.P. 761-3. 1986.

D. Archives

A 'summary account', of Kentish archives was compiled and published in 1914. This account is now very dated — especially the locations — but it still provides a useful overall survey:

CHURCHILL, IRENE JOSEPHINE. *A handbook to Kent records, containing a summary account of the principal classes of historical documents relating to the county, and a guide to their chief places of deposit.* Kent records 2. 1914.

Much more up to date information is provided by:

WRIGHT, DAVID. *East Kent parishes: a guide for genealogists, local historians and other researchers.* Whitstable: the author, 1991. Gazetteer with brief notes on records.

West Kent sources: a guide to family and local history research in the Diocese of Rochester. 2nd ed. Shirley: North West Kent Family History Society, 1994. Includes listing of resources by parish, notes on repositories, etc.

For Kentish parishes now part of London, much useful information may be found in:

WEBB, CLIFF. *My ancestors were Londoners: how can I find out more about them?* Society of Genealogists, 1996.

For a brief guide to a handful of major repositories, see:

BOURNE, SUSAN. *Six Kent repositories: a practical guide for the family historian.* 2nd ed. Northfleet: Susan Bourne, 1996. The repositories are: Centre for Kentish Studies, Canterbury Cathedral Archives, Rochester upon Medway Studies Centre, the Mormon library, the Institute of Heraldic and Genealogical Studies, and the University of Kent.

For repositories in S.E. London, formerly in Kent, see:

SILVERTHORNE, ELIZABETH, ed. *London local archives: a directory of local authority record offices and libraries.* 3rd ed. Guildhall Library/Greater London Archives Network, 1994. Includes, amongst others, repositories in the London Boroughs of Southwark, Greenwich, Lewisham, Bexley and Bromley.

Two articles provide up to date general information on sources:

CHALKLIN, C.W. 'Sources for Kentish history: trade and industry', *A.C.* **108,** 1991, 73-89. Not aimed at the genealogist, but nevertheless identifies many potentially useful sources.

CHURCHILL, ELSE. 'Sources for Kent', Family history 14(116), N.S., **92,** 1988, 301-11. List of manuscript notes by place.

A wide range of indexes to sources such as parish registers, probate records, census returns, *etc.,* are available. Many of these are unpublished. A listing is provided by:

BOURNE, SUSAN. *Indexes for the Kent family historian.* 2nd ed. Northfleet: the author, 1989.

E. *Centre for Kentish Studies*

This is the major archives repository for the county, formed from a number of institutions including the former Kent Archives Office. The archival holdings of the latter are listed in:

HULL, FELIX. *Guide to the Kent County Archives Office.* Maidstone: Kent County Council, 1958. Also available on 9 fiche as K.F.H.S.R.P. **677.** 1986 (filmed from the searchroom copy, which has extensive annotations). Supplemented by:

HULL, FELIX. *Guide to the Kent County Archives Office. First supplement 1957-1968.* Maidstone: Kent County Council, 1971. Also available on 5 fiche as K.F.H.S.R.P. **678.** 1986.

MELLING, ELIZABETH. *Guide to the Kent County Archives Office. Second supplement, 1969-1980.* Maidstone: Kent County Council, 1983. Also available on 5 fiche as K.F.H.S.R.P. **679.** 1986.

See also:

Twenty-five years: a report on the work of the Kent County Archives Office 1938-1958. Ashford: Headley Brothers, [1958?] Brief.

HULL, FELIX. 'The Kent Archives Office', *A.C.* **67-83,** 1954-69, *passim.* Lists accessions (now incorporated into the *Guides* listed above).

YATES, NIGEL. 'Kent Archives Office: major accessions, 1981-83', *A.C.* **101,** 1985, 313-47. Continuation of the guide and its two supplements.

YATES, NIGEL, SHAW, MAUREEN, & CARTER, MICHAEL. 'Kent Archives Office: major accessions, 1984-87', *A.C.* **105,** 1989, 251-85.

'Local archives of Great Britain, XI; the Kent Archives Office', *Archives* 2(13), 1955, 237-46.

'Kent Archives Office: genealogical information', *N.W.K.F.H.* 1(3), 1979, 72-3. Brief notes.

Many of the lists, indexes, calendars etc., compiled by the archivists, as well as large numbers of original documents, have been filmed by the Kent Family History Society and published in their *record publications* series. Fiche in this series are listed at appropriate points throughout this bibliography. The series includes a number of general calendars *etc:*

FREETH, S. *Catalogue of medieval fragments.* 1 fiche. K.F.H.S.R.P. **463.** 1986. In Kent Archives Office. Prepared in 1974, to be used with appendix to the 1958 edition of the *Guide to the Archives Office.*

K.A.O. unofficial document catalogue transcripts TR1885-TR2264. 3 fiche. K.F.H.S.R.P. **705.** 1986. For TR2270-TR2747, see **706.** (3 fiche)

C.K.S. unofficial document calendars U2823-U3057. 5 fiche. K.F.H.S.R.P. **1656.** 1992.

Catalogue, transcripts, photostats, microfilm and zerox copies of documents. 10 fiche. K.F.H.S.R.P. **703-4.** 1986.

4. JOURNALS AND NEWSPAPERS

A variety of historical and genealogical societies publish journals of interest to Kentish genealogists. The most useful are those emanating from the various family history societies. In addition to brief articles, these carry news of various society activities and — most importantly — list the names and addresses of members and the family names they are researching. Five family history societies at present issue journals:

Kent Family History Society journal. 1974- .

Folkestone Family History Society journal. 1978-84. Continued by *The Kentish connection: the journal of the Folkestone and District Family History Society.* 1985- .

North West Kent family history. [ ]: North West Kent Family History Society, 1978- .

Tunbridge Wells Family History Society [journal] 1991- .

The Woolwich and District Family History Society journal. 1980- .

Much more extensive articles are published in the county's principal historical journal:

Archaeologia Cantiana, being transactions of the Kent Archaeological Society. 1858- .

An index to all the many transcripts of documents published in *Archaeologia Cantiana* has been published on fiche:

POOLE, ERIC. *Transcripts of original documents in Archaeologia Cantiana: index.* 1 fiche. K.F.H.S.R.P. 43. 1985. Indexes all transcripts in vols. 1-99.

An extensive series of indexes has also been published in the journal:

FOX, RITA. 'General index to vols. I to XVIII of *Archaeologia Cantiana*', ed. W.A.Scott Robertson. *Archaeologia Cantiana* **19**, 1892, 1-313.

'Index of papers in *Archaeologia Cantiana*, vols XX to XXXV', *Archaeologia Cantiana* **36**, 1923, 167-76.

Archaeologia Cantiana: volume LII, being the general index to volumes XX to XLV. Kent Archaeological Society, 1940.

Archaeologia Cantiana volume LXVII, being the general index to volumes XLVI to LXIV. Ashford: Kent Archaeological Society, 1954.

STACE, A. *Archaeologia Cantiana, volume XC, being the general index to volumes LXV to LXXXVIII.* Ashford: Kent Archaeological Society, 1975.

DETSICAS, A.P. *Archaeologia Cantiana, volume XCIII, being the general index to volumes LXXXIX and XCI to CIX.* Stroud: Kent Archaeological Society, 1995.

See also:

PETERS, KEN. *Eynsford, Farningham, Lullingstone & Maplescombe: Archaeologia Cantiana references.* Publication **11**. [Farningham]: Farningham & Eynsford Local History Society, 1994.

Other county-wide journals include:

Bygone Kent: a monthly journal on all aspects of local history. Rainham: Meresborough Books, 1979- . Includes numerous brief articles, although few of strictly genealogical interest.

Cantium: a magazine of Kent local history. 6 vols. Dover: Thomas Becket Books, 1969-74.

Home counties magazine, devoted to the topography of London, Middlesex, Essex, Herts., Bucks., Berks., Surrey and Kent. 14 vols. F.E. Robinson & Co., 1899-1912. Indexed in *Home counties magazine: general index to volumes I-X.* G. Bell & Sons, [1911?].

The journal of Kent local history. Folkestone: Kent Council of Social Service, 1975- . For an index to vols. **1-28**, 1975-89, see **32**, 1991, 15-18. Re-titled *Journal of Kent history* from **32**, 1991- .

Kent records. New series. []: Kent Archaeological Society, 1990- . For the publication of original sources.

HOWELL, GEORGE O., ed. *The Kentish note book: a half-yearly magazine of notes, queries and replies on subjects connected with the county of Kent.* 2 vols. Gravesend: Smither Brothers, 1891-4. Many brief snippets of information.

Newspapers frequently contain useful genealogical information — especially in the births, marriages and death columns. For full listings of Kent newspapers, see:

BERGESS, WINIFRED A., & RIDDELL, BARBARA R.M., & WHYMAN, JOHN. *Bibliography of British newspapers: Kent.* British Library, 1982.

EAGLE, SELWYN, & DIXON, DIANA. *Newsplan: report of the Newsplan project in the London and South Eastern Library Region (LASER) January 1992 – December 1995.* British Library, 1996. Lists newspaper holdings in Bedfordshire, Berkshire, Buckinghamshire, Essex, Hertfordshire, Kent, Surrey and Sussex. See also:
TAYLER, BRIAN. *Maidstone journal 1786 index.* 1 fiche. K.F.H.S.R.P. **1197**. 1988.
HILTON, JOHN. *Index to the Maidstone journal: January-June 1831.* Kirkwall: the compiler, [199-]. Further volumes cover the rest of 1831, 1832, and July 1842 – June 1845. An index for 1786 is also available, but does not appear to be published.
A number of local historical societies publish transactions which include useful genealogical information. These include (amongst others):

Bromley
Bromley local history: aspects of the history of the community in the London Borough of Bromley, 1976- .

Cranbrook
The Cranbrook journal. Hawkhurst: Cranbrook Local History Society, 1988- .

Dartford
Transactions of the Dartford District Antiquarian Society. 9 vols. 1931-61.
Dartford Historical & Antiquarian Society newsletter. 1964- . For index, 1964-73, see **10**, 1973, 43-52; for 1974-83, **20**, 1983, 31-6.

Gravesend
The Gravesend Historical Society transactions. 1955- .

Greenwich
Transactions of the Greenwich Antiquarian Society ... 2 vols. 1905-14. Continued by: *Transactions of the Greenwich and Lewisham Antiquarian Society* ... 1924-90. Continued by: *Journal of the Greenwich Historical Society.* 1991- .
General index to the Transactions of the Greenwich and Lewisham Antiquarian Society, volumes I to VIII. The Society, 1981.

Lewisham
Lewisham Local History Society transactions. 1963-92. Continued by: *Lewisham history journal.* Lewisham Local History Society, 1993- .
'Lewisham Local History Society transactions master index', *Lewisham Local History Society transactions* 1986/87, 47-76.
See also Greenwich

Loose
Loose threads: journal of the Loose Area Research Group. 1988- .

Woolwich
Woolwich District Antiquarian Society annual report. 1894/5- . Sometimes referred to as: 'proceedings', 'transactions', or 'occasional papers'.
'A general index of the Woolwich District Antiquarian Society's proceedings, from vol. I (1894-5) to vol. XVII (1911-12)', *W.D.A.S.A.R.* **17**, 1912, 118-75.
WOOLWICH PUBLIC LIBRARIES. 'Woolwich District Antiquarian Society: index to proceedings volumes xviii to xxxi, inclusive, 1912-1958', *W.D.A.S.A.R.* **31**, 1958, [supplement].

Wye
Wye local history. Wye: Wye Historical Society, 1978- .

5. OCCUPATIONAL INFORMATION

Many works contain biographical information on people in particular occupations. Those relating to Kent are listed here, with certain exceptions. For clergymen, see below. section 11, for teachers and students, section 12, for M.Ps., sheriffs and other governmental officials, section 9. This list complements that in Raymond's *Occupational sources for genealogists,* which should be consulted for information on occupations nationally.

Actors
DAWSON, GILES E. *Records of plays and players in Kent: 1450-1642.* Malone Society collections **7**. 1965.

Airmen
BAXTER, G.C., OWEN, K.A., & BALDOCK, P. *Aircraft casualties in Kent, part 1: 1939 to 1940.* Rainham: Meresborough Books, 1990. Identifies all aircraft casualties and their crews.

Apothecaries
COUSINS, GERALD. 'Apothecaries & surgeons', *Cranbrook journal* **5**, 1992, 7-10. 17-18th c. names.

GUMLEY, VALDA F. 'Kent apothecaries 1 August 1815 − 31 July 1840', *K.F.H.S.J.* **6**(11), 1992, 378-82. List.

WHITTET, T. DOUGLAS. 'Kent apothecaries' and barber-surgeons' tokens and their issues', *A.C.* **103**, 1987, 69-78. Includes biographical information.

Apprentices
St. Leonard, Deal: apprenticeship indentures 1661-1788. 10 fiche. K.F.H.S.R.P. **402**. 1986. Filmed from the original manuscripts, with a calender.

See also Masters and Watermen

Architects
The year book of the South Eastern Society of Architects ... 1929. Eastbourne: Baskerville Press, 1929. Lists members.

Architecture in Kent, Surrey & Sussex: the year book of the South-Eastern Society of Architects ... 1937/8-1940/1. Lists members.

Armourers
SHARP, ARTHUR D. 'The story of the Greenwich armoury', *T.G.L.A.S.* 3(4), 1929, 151-65. Includes list of armourers.

Artists
ELLISTON-ERWOOD, F.C. 'Notes on local artists', *W.D.A.S.A.R.* **25**, 1935, 16-25.

FRY, CYRIL. 'Artists in Greenwich and Lewisham', *T.G.L.A.S.* 7(6), 1972, 278-89. Includes list of 'local exhibitors at Royal Academy 1769-1904'.

'Artists of Gravesend up to the end of the 19th century', *Gravesend Historical Society transactions* **10**, 1964, 7-22.

Athletes
SAUNDERS, D.K., & WEEKS-PEARSON, A.J., *The centenary history of the Blackheath harriers.* Blackheath: Blackheath Harriers, 1971. Many names of runners.

Authors
HANDLEY-TAYLOR, GEOFFREY. *Kent authors today, being a checklist of authors born in Kent ...* Eddison Press, 1973.

Directory of writers in the South-East of England. 2nd ed. Tunbridge Wells: South East Arts Association, 1977.

Kentish books, Kentish writers. [ ]: Kent County Library, 1969. Brief biographical dictionary (pamphlet).

Bank Customers
Shepherdswell [Sibertswold], Kent: Penny Bank ledger, 1859-1869. 3 fiche. K.F.H.S.R.P. **343**. 1986. Filmed from the original ledger.

Bankers
SENCICLE, LORRAINE A.M. *Banking on Dover.* Dover: Powell Print, 1993. Includes information on the Fector, Latham and Minet families *etc.,* bankers of Dover.

Bankrupts
GUMLEY, VALDA I. 'Kent bankrupts, 1st January 1774 − 30th June 1786', *K.F.H.S.J.* **6**(6), 1991, 197-9. See also **6**(8), 1991, 258.

HOLMES, SUE. 'Bankrupts', *W.D.F.H.S.J.* **51**, 1993, 2-3. List for Woolwich area, from the *Kentish Independent,* 1854.

MELLING, ELIZABETH. 'Kentish tradesmen in the early nineteenth century', *Society of Local Archivists bulletin* **12**, 1953, 30-33. Discussion of archives relating to insolvent debtors.

Barge Builders
SATTIN, D.L. *Barge building amd barge builders of the Swale.* Gillingham: Meresborough Books, 1990.

Bargemen
WILLMOTT, FRANK G. *Cement, mud, and muddies: a history of A.P.C.M. barges.* Rainham: Meresborough Books, 1977. Includes information on bargemen.

Biscuit Bakers
BIRCHENOUGH, JOSEPHINE. 'Deptford Victualling Yard, (c. 1760)', *N.W.K.F.H.* **6**(4), 1992/3, 116-8. Primarily concerns biscuit bakers.

Book Trades
GOULDEN, RICHARD. *The Faversham book trade, 1730-1900.* Faversham papers **51**. Faversham: Faversham Society, 1996. Biographical dictionary of printers, publishers, booksellers *etc.*
HETHERINGTON, KEITH. 'Printers and publishers of Tunbridge Wells', *B.K.* **7**(8), 1986, 451-6. 19-20th c.
KNOTT, DAVID. *The book trade in Kent: working paper: Isle of Thanet directory, c.1778 to 1838.* Reading: privately printed, 1989.

Brewers
HETHERINGTON, K. 'Some prominent Kent brewers', *B.K.* **3**(11), 1982, 677-82; **7**(9), 1986, 529-34. Brief biographical notes.
'Common brewers in Greenwich, Deptford and Lewisham in the last 200 years', *T.G.L.A.S.* **8**(3), 1975, 114-5. List.

Brickmakers
CUFLEY, DAVID. 'Woolwich & Plumstead brickmakers', *W.D.F.H.S.J.* **50**, 1993, 2-7. 19th c.

Building Tradesmen
KIRBY, J.W. 'Builders work at Placentia, 1543-1544', *T.G.L.A.S.* **4**(6), 1952-3, 285-307. Accounts with many names of building tradesmen at Greenwich.

Cardmakers
SINGLETON, TONY. 'Cardmakers & wiredrawers', *Cranbrook journal* **5**, 1992, 19-21. 16-17th c.

Carriers
'Public locomotion in Kent 100 years ago', *Kent magazine* **1**, 1896, 280-6. Includes 'list of carriers of the *Kentish gazette,* 1798'.

Clockmakers
HERBERT, ADRIAN. 'Dartford watch and clockmakers between 1721 and 1922', *Dartford Historical & Antiquarian Society newsletter* **27**, 1990, 21-8.

Coastguards
STAGE, EILEEN. 'Index of coastguards: reflecting the history of anti-smuggling', *N.W.K.F.H.* **4**(3), 1986, 98-100.
See also Customs Officers

Cricket Bat Makers
AVIS, L.D. 'Cricket bat & ball makers from the 1881 Southborough census', *K.F.H.S.J.* **7**(7), 1994, 234; **8**(6), 1997, 280; **8**(7), 1997, 343-4. List.

Cricketers
BAKER, THOMAS HENRY. *History of the Cobham Cricket Club, from its foundation in 1850 to the close of the season of 1898.* Rochester: W.T. Wildish, 1899. Many names.
BENNETT, WALTER. *Sidcup Cricket Club 1877-1977: a history and reference book.* [Sidcup]: Sidcup Cricket Club, 1977. Includes many names of cricketers.
DREW, BERNARD. *A hundred years of Farningham cricket.* Gravesend: Gravesend and Dartford Reporter, 1957. Includes list of playing members, 1870-1914.

HARRIS, G.R.C., ed. *The history of Kent County Cricket* ... Eyre & Spottiswoode, 1907.

HARRIS, G.R.C., & ASHLEY-COOPER, F.S. *Kent Cricket matches 1719-1880.* Canterbury: Gibbs & Sons, 1929.

HAYES, DEAN. *Kent cricketing greats: 53 of the best cricketers for Kent, 1869-1989.* Tunbridge Wells: Spellmount, 1990.

HILL, ROGER. *History of Bexley Cricket Club.* 2 vols. Harrow: Frank Richards, 1990. Many names. Vol. 2 gives biographies of club presidents.

MILTON, HOWARD. *Kent cricket records 1815-1993, incorporating all first-class matches 1864 to 1993, and all important matches 1815 to 1863.* Royston: Limlow Books, 1994.

MOORE, DUDLEY. *The history of Kent County Cricket Club.* Christopher Helm, 1988. Includes 'biographical details of Kent players'.

NORMAN, PHILIP. *Scores and annals of the West Kent Cricket Club, originally the Prime's Plain Club, with some account of the neighbourhoods of Chislehurst and Bromley and of the families residing there.* Eyre & Spottiswoode 1897.

OSBORN, T. *The history of the Mote Cricket Club 1857-1981: the first 125 years.* [ ]: Kent County Library, 1990. Includes lists of officers, many notes on personalities, and some portraits.

Criminals

GRAY, ADRIAN. *Crime and criminals in Victorian Kent.* Gillingham: Meresborough Books, 1985.

Customs Officers

CARSON, EDWARDS A. 'The customs records of the Kent ports: a survey', *Journal of the Society of Archivists* 4, 1970-74, 31-44. Discussion and list of records which identify customs officers, ships' masters, merchants, *etc.*

NIELD, BOB. '1841 census: customs and coastguard officers, Folkestone, Kent', *K.C.* 4(10), 1988, 267-71. For 1851, see 5(1), 1988, 7-11; 5(2), 1988, 36-41; 5(3), 1988, 70-74. For 1861, see 5(4), 1989, 100-105, 5(5), 1990, 136-42; 5(6), 1987, 172-9. For 1871, see 5(7), 1990, 202-7; 5(8), 1990, 235-44; 5(9), 1990, 269-72. For 1881, see 5(10), 1990, 293-300; 6(1), 1991, 6-13.

Dairymen

HERBERT, ADRIAN. 'The cowkeepers and dairy people of Dartford', *Dartford Historical & Antiquarian Society newsletter* 23, 1986, 6-24. Many names mentioned.

Dockers

BIRCHENOUGH, JOSEPHINE. 'Working Deptford in the 18th century', *N.W.K.F.H.* 6(6), 1993, 188-90. Brief note on dockyard employees.

GREEN, HENRY. 'Staff of the Woolwich Dockyard', *W.D.F.H.S.J.* 15, 1983, 5-7. List, 1819.

Dredgermen

See Fishermen

Farmers

SELBY, PRIDEAUX GEORGE. *The Faversham Farmers' Club and its members.* Faversham: Voile & Roberson, 1927. Includes extensive biographies of members.

Firemen

THOMAS, B.G. *Fire-fighting in Maidstone.* Phillimore & Co., 1976. Includes list of chief fire officers from 1873.

Fishermen

COOMBE, DEREK. *The Bawleymen: fishermen and dredgermen of the River Medway.* Rainham: Perrant Books, 1979. General study; includes list of 'freemen and apprentices of the Rochester Oyster & Floating Fishery', 1978.

LUDLOW, BARBARA. 'Fishermen of Greenwich', *W.D.F.H.S.J.* 50, 1993, 10-22. Includes a list, 18-19th c.

Footballers

RHIND, NEIL. 'Blackheath Football Club, 1862-1870: an investigation into its origins, and some notes on the early years', *T.G.L.A.S.* 10(1), 1985, 21-45. Includes list of members.

SAUNDERS, D.D. *The old bird and the cherry pickers: a century of soccer in Hawkhurst.* Hawkhurst: Wealden Advertisers, 1990. Includes various lists of footballers and club officials.

TRIGGS, ROGER. *Priestfield profiles: a who's who of Gillingham's football league players, 1950-1988.* Gillingham: Roger Triggs, 1988.

Freemasons

LUSTY, D. WILLIAM, & WILLIAMS, E.M.P. *History of Kent Lodge no. 15, 1752-1952.* D.G. Lusty & Son, [1952?] Includes lists of masters, treasurers, and secretaries, and of members in 1951-2.

POCKNELL, E. *A short history of the Hervey Lodge, in 1692, of the United and Honourable Fraternity of Antient Free and Accepted Masons of England ...* [ ]: The Lodge, 1937. Includes list of members.

A short history of the first fifty years of the William Russell Chapter no. 1314, 1904-1954. Privately published, [1954?] Includes list of members (freemasons).

Gasmen

ELLISTON-ERWOOD, F.C. 'The directors and officers of the Woolwich Consumers Gas Co., 1870', *W.D.A.S.A.R.* **25**, 1935, 26-8. Notes on a photograph.

Golfers

FLYNN, JOHN, ed. *A century of golf on Dartford Heath, 1891-1991.* [Dartford]: Dartford Golf Club, 1991. Includes various lists of golfers *etc.*

HUGHES, W.E., ed. *Chronicles of Blackheath golfers, with illustration and portraits.* Chapman and Hall, 1897. Includes 'lists of officers, and of medal and cup winners'.

Gunfounders

TOMLINSON, H.C. 'Wealden gunfounding: an analysis of its demise in the eighteenth century', *Economic history review* 2nd series **29**, 1976, 383-400. General study of Kent, Surrey and Sussex; includes some names of ironmasters.

Gunpowder Manufacturers

WEST, JENNY. *Gunpowder, government and war in the mid-eighteenth century.* Studies in history **63**. Boydell for the Royal Historical Society, 1991. Includes list of 'Gunpowder mills supplying the Ordnance Office in the mid-eighteenth century', naming many gunpowder manufacturers.

Gypsies
See Vagrants

Hockey Players

EAMES, GEOFFREY L. *A history of Bromley Hockey Club 1888-1963.* Bromley: Harry Dawson, 1963. Includes names of officers, *etc.*

Hop Token Issuers

ACWORTH, R.W.H. *Hop tokens in Kent.* Folkestone: Kent Council of Social Services, [1937?] Includes list of 110 tokens, with many names of issuers.

HENDERSON, ALAN C. *Hop tokens of Kent and Sussex & their issuers.* Spink, 1990.

Huntsmen

'Game Acts', *N.W.K.F.H.* **3**(5), 1984, 158-61. List of persons licensed to take game *(not* gamekeepers) 1818.

Informers

MONSON, LESLIE. 'Common informers in Greenwich and Deptford, 1763', *T.G.L.A.S.* **107**(4), 1988, 179-88.

Innkeepers

BUCKINGHAM, CHRISTOPHER. 'A directory of Kent taverns, 1636', *Cantium* **6**(1), 1974, 7-11. List of innkeepers.

WINSTANLEY, M. 'The rural publican and his business in East Kent before 1914', *Oral history* **4**(2), 1976, 63-78.

Bexley

PACKER, JAMES. *Bexley pubs: the history of your local.* Bexley: London Borough of Bexley Libraries & Museums Dept., 1995. Traces the descent of pubs, giving many names of publicans.

Chatham

HARRIS, EDWIN. *Chatham inns and signs.* Eastgate series **22**. Rochester Harris, 1914. Includes names of innkeepers from an 1838 directory, *etc.*

Dartford

BAKER, CHRIS. 'Dartford's drinking establishments in 1886', *Dartford Historical & Antiquarian Society newsletter* **23**, 1986, 24-8. List of 60 innkeepers *etc.*

See also St. Mary Cray

Farningham

BLACK, SHIRLEY BURGOYNE. 'Farningham inns and innkeepers of the turnpike road era', *N.W.K.F.H.* **3**(8), 1984, 267-74.

Folkestone

KILLICK, JENNIE. 'Folkestone publicans', *K.C.* **9**(2), 1995 37-8. List extracted from Folkestone sessions papers, 1817.

Rochester

AVELING, S.T. 'Rochester inns', *A.C.* **21**, 1895, 315-26. Extracts from deeds *etc.*, relating to innkeepers, 15-17th c.

St. Mary Cray

WHYLER, FRED. 'Victuallers recognizances, 1605', *N.W.K.F.H.* **1**(7), 1980, 195-7. List of those entered into at St. Mary Cray and Dartford.

Ironmasters

BROWN, RUTH R. 'Wealden ironmasters and the Board of Ordnance after 1770', *Wealden iron: bulletin of the Wealden Iron Research Group* 2nd series **14**, 1994, 31-47. Extracts from Board of Ordnance records, giving many names of ironmasters, gunfounders, *etc.*

GORING, J.J. 'Wealden ironmasters in the age of Elizabeth', in IVES, E.W., KNECHT, R.J., & SCARISBRICK, J.J., eds. *Wealth and power in Tudor England: essays presented to S.T. Bindoff.* Athlone, 1978, 204-27. Includes list.

STRAKER, ERNEST. *Wealden iron: a monograph on the former ironworks in the counties of Sussex, Surrey and Kent, comprising a history of the industry from the earliest times to its cessation, together with a topographical survey of the existing remains from personal observation.* G. Bell & Sons, 1931. Includes names of many ironmasters.

TEESDALE, EDMUND. 'The 1574 lists of ironworks in the Weald: a re-examination', *Wealden iron: Bulletin of the Wealden Iron Research Group* 2nd series **6**, 1986, 7-41. Lists ironmasters.

Lighthouse Keepers

NICOL, RUTH. 'Children of lighthouse keepers at South Foreland', *K.F.H.S.J.* **5**(6), 1988, 220-21. From the register of the National School at Cliffe.

Martyrs

MILLER, G. ANDERSON. *Noble martyrs of Kent.* Marshall Morgan & Scott, [1924]. Biographical notes on Protestant martyrs.

Masters

BARTLETT, A.E., ed. *Kent masters and their apprentices, 1763-1774.* 2 fiche. K.F.H.S.R.P. **24**. 1984.

BARTLETT, A.E., ed. *Canterbury masters and their apprentices, 1763-1777, with a few entries of 1758-1762.* Canterbury: Harrington Family Miscellany Record Publications, 1978. List 650 masters and their apprentices.

DAVIES, PETER. 'Some early Folkestone masters & apprentices', *K.C.* **8**(2), 1994, 44. Late 18th c., from Inland Revenue registers.

GREEN, E.R., ed *Gravesend and Milton masters and apprentices 1636-1834.* Gravesend: privately published, 1984.

Medical Personnel

HALL, F. MARCUS, STEVENS, RICHARD S., & WHYMAN, JOHN. *The Kent and Canterbury Hospital, 1790-1987.* Canterbury: Kent Postgraduate Medical Centre, 1987. Includes lists of medical staff; also of chaplains.

GREEN, HENRY. 'The Royal Hospital, Greenwich, establishment (1819)', *W.D.F.H.S.J.* **12**, 1982, 5-7. List of staff.

POLAND, JOHN. *Records of the Miller Hospital and Royal Kent Dispensary.* Greenwich: H. Richardson, 1893. Includes lists of officers.

MAXWELL, THEODORE. 'Early Woolwich doctors', *W.D.A.S.A.R.* **13**, 1908, 100-5. General discussion.

See also Nurses

Merchants

See Customs Officers

Millers

FULLER, M.J. *The watermills of the East Malling and Wateringbury streams.* Maidstone: Christine Swift Bookshops, 1980.

Monumental Masons

GUNNIS, RUPERT. 'Signet monuments in Kentish churches', *A.C.* **62**, 1950, 57-86. Biographical dictionary of monumental masons.

Nurses

KEYMER, BILL. 'Nurses in the Royal Hospital, Greenwich in 1851', *W.D.F.H.S.J.* **25**, 1986, 10-11.

Kent Voluntary Aid Detachments: report of hospitals and detachments 1914-1919. Bromley: S. Bush & Son, 1920. Lists volunteer nurses *etc.*

Papermakers

ROOME, K.M. 'Some papermakers of Dartford', *J.K.L.H.* **38**, 1994, 12-13. Brief.

Pilots

HARRIS, G.G. *The Trinity House of Deptford, 1514-1660.* Athlone Press, 1969. Include lists of masters and elder brethren.

HOLLINGSBEE, KATHLEEN. 'Cinque Ports pilots of Dover, Deal, and Thanet', *K.F.H.S.J.* 4(11), 1986, 392-3. Includes list of pilots, 1788.

Pipemakers

WILLIAMS, D.E. 'Clay tobacco pipes from Chatham', *A.C.* **95**, 1980, 231-40. See also **96**, 1981, 368-9. Includes list of pipemakers, 17-20th c.

'Pipemakers', *N.W.K.F.H.* 3(1), 1983, 19. Brief list for Dartford and Gravesend area. 1697-1880.

Postmen

BATHE, PETER. 'Postal history of Woolwich', *Woolwich and District Antiquarian Society proceeding* **37**, 1983, 8-23.

DONALD, ARCHIE. *The posts of Sevenoaks in Kent: an account of the handling and transportation of the written communication of Sevenoaks District (Westerham to Wrotham, Biggin Hill to Edenbridge) on the road to Rye and Hastings.* Tenterden: Woodvale Press, 1992. Lists postmasters.

MUGGERIDGE, SIDNEY J. *The postal history of Maidstone and the surrounding villages, with notes on their postal markings.* Special series publication **28**. Postal History Society, 1972. Includes list of Maidstone postmasters, 1667-1970.

Printers and Publishers

See Book Trades

Railwaymen

AVIS, L.D. 'Extracts from the 1881 Tonbridge census', *K.F.H.S.J.* 6(8), 1991, 264-5. Relating to railwaymen.

'Railway workers in Tonbridge 1881', *K.F.H.S.J.* 7(7), 1994, 234. List.

Royal Arsenal

'Arsenal workers', *W.D.F.H.S.J.* **5**, 1981, 14-17. List of employees at Woolwich Arsenal, 1776-7.

GREEN, HENRY J. 'Fragments of the Royal Woolwich Arsenal', *W.D.F.H.S.J.* **28**, 1987, 9-11. Includes list of staff, early 19th c.

GREEN, HENRY. 'Staff of the Royal Laboratory', *W.D.F.H.S.J.* **14**, 1983, 6-8. At Woolwich, 1819.

GREEN, HENRY. 'Central staff at the Royal Arsenal, 1898', *W.D.F.H.S.J.* **33**, 1988, 7-8. List.

Seamen

BRUNTON, ANN,& GODFREY, BARBARA. 'Royal Alfred Institution for old seamen, Belvedere', *N.W.K.F.H.* 6(6), 1993, 191-2. 1891 census listing of retired merchant seamen from many parts of England.

GREEN, H. 'Staff of the Royal Naval College, 1881', *W.D.F.H.S.J.* **37**, 1990, 15-16. List.

HIGHLEY, SUE. 'Volunteers or press-ganged?' *W.D.F.H.S.J.* **59**, 1995, 3. List naval 'volunteers' from Greenwich, 1795.

KELLY, DOREEN. 'A list of the ships company belonging to H.M. hired lugger 'Rover', *K.C.* 4(5), 1987, 109-13. 1800.

MCGURK, J.J.N. 'A levy of seamen in the Cinque Ports, 1602', *Mariners mirror* **66**, 1980, 137-44. Discussion based on potentially useful sources.

RICKARD, GILLIAN. *Kent enrolments under the Navy Act, 1796.* Canterbury: Gillian Rickard, 1996. Lists 461 men recruited as sailors.

'Register of protections from being pressed', *K.C.* 4(2), 1986, 36-8; 4(3), 1986, 66-70; 4(4), 1986, 92-7. Lists 'protections' given to masters of ships.

See also Customs Officers

Shipbuilders

BANBURY, PHILIP. *Shipbuilders of the Thames and Medway.* Newton Abbot: David & Charles, 1971. Traces the history of both the Royal Dockyards and many private shipyards; identifies numerous shipbuilders.

Silk Weavers

ROTHSTEIN, N.K. 'Canterbury and London: the silk industry in the late seventeenth century', *Textile history* **20**, 1989, 33-47. Includes lists of Canterbury silk weavers and London silk factors.

Skinners

PEARCE, K. 'The skinners of Woolwich', *W.D.F.H.S.J.* **42**, 1991, 5-8. 19th c.

Smugglers

MUSKETT, P. 'Deal smugglers in the eighteenth century', *Southern history* **8**, 1986, 46-72.

WAUGH, MARY. *Smuggling in Kent and Sussex, 1700-1840.* Newbury: Countryside Books, 1985. Includes notes on leading smugglers.

Soldiers and Militiamen

SCOTT, JAMES R. 'Paylist of the forces, raised in Kent, to resist the Spanish invasion, 1588', *A.C.* **11**, 1877, 388-91.

A. *By Place*

Birchington

ROBERTSON, W.A. SCOTT. 'Archaeological notes on Thanet: Birchington', *A.C.* **12**, 1828, 402-9. Includes muster roll, 1614, and list of soldiers billeted in the parish, 1627, *etc.*

Bromley

WHYLER, FRED. 'Militia: some aspects', *N.W.K.F.H.* **4**(10), 1988, 368-73. Lists of cavalry raised by Bromley, 1796, and of 'inspectors of hundreds, superintendants of parishes, special constables, and providers of carriages and carts' for the Hundreds of Bromley, Beckenham and Ruxley.

Charing

HULL, FELIX. 'An early Kentish militia roll', *A.C.* **68**, 1955, 159-66. Roll of 1415 for Charing, Egerton and Smarden.

Faversham

DANE, HERBERT. *The war years, 1939-1945 in Faversham and district: a record of the activities and service of its people in the national effort, with the roll of honour commemorating those who gave their lives in the cause of liberty.* Faversham: F. Austin & Sons, [195-?]

Folkestone

'Men of Folkestone who gave their lives during the Great War 1914-18', *F.F.H.S.J.* 2(6), 1982, 80; 2(7), 1982, 93; 2(8), 1982, 103; 2(9), 1982, 122; 2(10), 1983, 133; 3(1), 1983, 10; 3(2), 1983, 22; 3(3), 1983, 40 & 46. List from chapter 14 of *Folkestone during the war.*

Margate

JACOB, KENNETH W. *Muster rolls, Aug. 1599, Ss. John and Peter, Thanet & Birchington.* 1 fiche. K.F.H.S.R.P. **1114**. 1987.

Rochester

ALLEN, COLIN. *Transcript with index of the 1821 militia ballot list for the parish of St. Margaret, Rochester, Kent.* Privately published, 1995.

Saint Peter in Thanet

ROBERTSON, W.A. SCOTT. 'Archaeological notes on Thanet: St. Peters', *A.C.* **12**, 1878, 388-91. Includes list of soldiers billeted in the parish, 1628, muster roll, 1619, *etc.* *See also* Margate

Sandgate

'Sandgate Great War dead', *K.C.* 3(10), 1985, 215. List.

Sandgate Castle

RUTTON, WILLIAM LOFTIE. 'Sandgate Castle', *A.C.* **21**, 1895, 244-59. Includes list of captains and lieutenants, 17-19th c., with biographical notes.

Woolwich

HOGG, O.F.G. *The Royal Arsenal: its background, origin and subsequent history.* 2 vols. Oxford University Press, 1963. Extensive; includes various lists of officers and employees, *etc.*

HOLMES, SUE. 'Soldiers at Woolwich',
W.D.F.H.S.J. **59,** 1995, 25-7. List of
regiments stationed at Woolwich, 1851-89.

B. *Regimental Histories, etc*

18th Kent Rifle Volunteer Corps
LANGRIDGE, BARRY. '18th Kent
(Bromley) Rifle Volunteer Corps',
N.W.K.F.H. **7**(3), 1995, 74-7. Brief
account, 19-20th c., from a genealogical
viewpoint.

Chatham and Gillingham Volunteer Artillery
DOUCH, JOHN. 'Medway muster roll',
K.F.H.S.J. **6**(4), 1990, 118-9. Roll of the
Chatham and Gillingham Volunteer
Artillery, 1807.

Earl of Ulster's Regiment
CHAPLIN, H.D. *The 97th, or Earl of Ulster's
Regiment, 1824- 1881.* Maidstone: Queens
Own Royal West Kent Regimental
Museum Committee, 1973. Includes
various lists of names.

East Kent Volunteers
IGGLESDEN, CHARLES. *History of the East
Kent Volunteers.* Kentish Express
(Igglesden & Co.), 1899. Many names, 18-
19th c.

East Kent Yeomanry
HARRIS, G.R.C. *A century of Yeoman service:
records of the East Kent Yeomanry (the
Royal East Kent Mounted Rifles).*
Ashford: Kentish Express, 1899. Includes
roll of officers.

Gentlemen and Yeomanry Cavalry
WEBB, P., & WEIR, N. *Sussex, Hampshire,
Surrey and Kent War Office list 1804:
list of officers of the Gentlemen and
Yeomanry Cavalry and Volunteer
Infantry.* 1 fiche Eastbourne: PBN
Publications, 1995.

Kent Home Guard
GULVIN, KEITH R. *Kent Home Guard: a
history.* Rochester: North Kent Books,
1980. Mentions many names.

Kent Yeomanry
LUSHINGTON, FRANK. *Yeoman service: a
short history of the Kent Yeomanry 1939-
1945.* Media Society, 1947. Includes roll of
honour, *etc.*

Royal East Kent Regiment
*Historical records of the Buffs (Royal East
Kent Regiment), 3rd Foot, formerly
designated the Holland Regiment, and
Prince George of Denmark's Regiment.*
Media Society, et al, 1922-51. Contents:
v.1. 1572-1704, by H.R.Knight; v.2. 1704-
1814, by C.R.B.Knight; v.3. 1814-1914, by
C.R.B.Knight; v.4. 1914-1919, by
R.H.S.Moody; v.5. 1919-1948, by
C.R.B.Knight. Includes various lists of
names.
*Soldiers died in the Great War
1914-19, part 8: The Buffs (East Kent
Regiment).* Polstead: J.B.Hayward & Son,
1989. Originally published 1921.
BLAXLAND, GREGORY. *The farewell years:
the final historical records of the Buffs,
Royal East Kent Regiment (3rd Foot)
formerly designated the Holland
Regiment and Prince George of
Denmark's Regiment, 1948-1967.*
Canterbury: Queens' Own Buffs Office,
1967. Includes various brief lists of
names.

Royal West Kent Regiment
CHAPLIN, HOWARD DOUGLAS. *The Queen's
Own Royal West Kent Regiment, 1881-
1914.* Maidstone: The Regimental History
Committee, 1959. Includes roll of honour,
1881-1913.
ATKINSON, C.T. *The Queen's Own Royal
West Kent Regiment, 1914-1919.* Simpkin,
Marshall, Hamilton, Kent & Co., 1924.
Includes various extensive lists of names.
Indexed in: *Name index to the book 'The
Queen's Own Royal West Kent Regiment,
1914-1919.* fiche. North West Kent Family
History Society, 1996. Not seen.
*The history of the Eighth Battalion, the
Queen's Own Royal West Kent
Regiment, 1914-1919.* Hazell Watson &
Viney, 1921. Includes list of honours and
awards.

RUSSELL, R.O. *The history of the 11th (Lewisham) Battalion the Queen's Own Royal West Kent Regiment.* Lewisham Newspaper Co., 1934. Includes roll of honour, 1914-18.

Soldiers died in the Great War 1914-1919 part 53: The Queen's Own (Royal West Kent Regiment). Polstead: J.B. Hayward & Son 1989. Originally published 1921.

CHAPLIN, HOWARD DOUGLAS. *The Queen's Own Royal West Kent Regiment, 1920-1950.* Michael Joseph, 1954. Includes roll of honour, 1939-1945.

CLARKE, E.B. STANLEY, & TILLOTT, A.T. *From Kent to Kohima: being the history of the 4th Battalion, the Queen's Own West Kent Regiment (T.A.) 1939-47.* Aldershot: Gale and Polden, 1951. Includes roll of those who 'proceeded overseas" in March 1940.

West Kent Militia

BONHOTE, J. *Historical records of the West Kent Militia with some account of the earlier defensive levies in Kent.* Hudson & Kearns, 1909. Re-published on 11 fiche, K.F.H.S.R.P. **436.** 1986. Numerous lists of names, 16-19th c.

West Kent Yeomanry

EDMEADES, J.F. *Some historical records of the West Kent (Q.O.) Yeomanry, 1794-1909.* Andrew Melrose, 1909. Includes 'list of present and past officers ...'

HOLMES, SUE. 'Muster rolls', *W.D.F.H.S.J.* **17,** 1984, 13- 19. Roll of the West Kent Queen's Own Yeomanry Cavalry, 1890.

PONSONBY, CHARLES. *West Kent (Q.O.) Yeomanry and 10th (Yeomanry) Batt. the Buffs, 1914-1919.* Andrew Melrose, 1920. Includes various rolls of officers and men.

Theatrical Personnel

MORLEY, MALCOLM. *Margate and its theatres, 1730-1965.* Museum Press, 1966. Many names; includes list of managers and pedigree of Thorne, 19-20th c.

See also Actors

Trade Unionists

FINCHER, SALLY. 'Trade Union records', *K.F.H.S.J.* **5**(2), 1987, 71-2. Brief discussion using Kent records.

Tradesmen

MELLING, ELIZABETH. 'Kentish tradesmen in the early nineteenth century', *A.C.* **66,** 1954, 98-102. Note on a collection of account books and papers of insolvent debtors at Kent Archives Office.

RAWLING, JEAN. 'Names of tradesmen of Orpington & District extracted from the registers of All Saints parish church, 1783-1799', *N.W.K.F.H.* **6**(11), 1994, 367.

In an age when small coin was in short supply, many tradesmen issued their own tokens. Studies of these provide many names of tradesmen. See:

HAMMOND, J.A. 'Eighteenth century halfpenny tokens of Kent', in *Woolwich & District Antiquarian Society occasional papers* **3,** 1970, 13-21.

HAMMOND, J.A. 'Woolwich coins, tokens and medals', *W.D.A.S.A.R.* **33,** 1967, 55-7.

'Notes on the 18th century tokens of Kent', *The Kentish note book* **1-2,** 1891-2, *passim.*

TILLEY, ERNEST W. 'The seventeenth-century token issuers of Gravesend and Milton-next-Gravesend', *A.C.* **85,** 1970, 149-74. General discussion.

WATERS, ARTHUR WILLIAM. *The token coinage of South London issued in the 18th and 19th centuries.* Leamington Spa: Simmons & Waters, 1904.

RHODES, N.G. 'Seventeenth-century token of South-East Kent', *K.C.* **5**(6), 1990, 161-3. List.

BALDWIN, A.H. 'Notes on the 18th century tokens of Kent', *Kentish note book* **1-2,** 1891-4, *passim.*

Vagrants

RICKARD, GILLIAN. *Vagrants, gypsies and travellers in Kent, 1572-1948.* Canterbury: the author, 1995. Includes a comprehensive listing of surviving records, mainly from parish records and quarter session, *etc.*

Watermen

COTTRELL, ROBERT J. *Surname index to the Company of Watermen & Lightermen, London.* 21 fiche + folders. Bexleyheath: R.J. Cottrell, [199-?]. Includes apprentices, 1700-1884; includes many from Kent.

KEYMER, FAITH. 'Member of the Watermen & Lightermen's Company', *W.D.F.H.S.J.* **31,** 1988, 8-12; **32,** 1988, 8-11. List of apprentices bound in 1860 from Charlton, Deptford, Erith, Greenwich, Plumstead and Woolwich; also list of affidavits for 1840.

Wire Drawers
See Cardmakers

Witches
EWEN, C.L'ESTRANGE, ed. *Witch hunting and witch trials: the indictments for witchcraft from records of 1,373 assizes held for the Home Circuit, A.D. 1559-1736.* Kegan Paul, Trench, Trubner & Co., 1929. Primarily concerned with Essex, Kent and Surrey.

6. TRADE DIRECTORIES AND MAPS

A. *Directories*

Trade directories are invaluable sources for locating people in nineteenth and early twentieth-century England. They performed a similar function to the modern telephone directory, and frequently list local inhabitants by street, as well as providing much useful general information. There are many directories for Kent; the list which follows is selective and, in the main, only includes items which have actually been seen. The essential guide to Kentish directories, which provides locations in local libraries is:

BERGESS, WINIFRED F., & RIDDELL, BARBARA M. *Kent directories located.* 2nd ed. [ ]. Kent County Library, 1978.
Directories covering the whole county include (in chronological order):

Pigot and Co's royal national and commercial directory and topography of the counties of Kent, Surrey and Sussex ... J. Pigot & Co., 1839. Facsimile reprint Kings Lynn: Michael Winton, 1993.

BAGSHAW, SAMUEL. *History, gazetteer and directory of the County of Kent ...* 2 vols. Sheffield: G.Ridge, 1847. Re-published on 21 fiche, Maidstone: Kent County Council, [199-?].

Melville & Co's. directory & gazetteer of Kent, containing a descriptive account of each city, town and village, followed by a directory. F.R. Melville & Co., 1858. Re-published on 8 fiche, Maidstone: Kent County Council, [199-?].

Post Office directory of Essex, Herts., Middlesex, Kent, Surrey & Sussex. Kelly & Co., 1862-78. 5 issues. Continued by *Kelly's directory of the six home counties.* 2 vols. Kelly and Co., 1882. Continued by: *Kelly's directory of Kent, Surrey & Sussex.* Kelly and Co., 1887-1938. 19 issues. The Kent portion was also issued separately as *The Post Office directory of Kent,* or *Kelly's directory of Kent.* Many issues have been filmed and re-published on fiche by Kent County Council, and also for the *British Isles directories* series published Albert Park, Victoria: Nick Vine Hall, 199- .

J.G. Harrod and Co's., postal and commercial directory of Kent and Sussex. J.C. Harrod and Co., 1867. Re-published on 18 fiche, Maidstone: Kent County Council, [199-?].

Green's mid-Kent court guide, gazetteer and county blue book: a fashionable register and general survey of the county ... Green & Co., 1874. Re-published on 10 fiche, Maidstone: Kent County Council, [199-?].

Kent, Surrey and Sussex directory, 1935[-1938/9]. Walsall: Aubrey & Co., 1935-9. 4 vols.

Suburban Kent

Pigot and Co's. A directory of London and its suburbs ... J. Pigot & Co., 1839. Reprinted Kings Lynn: Michael Winton, 1993. Includes N.W. Kent.

Post Office London directory ... Frederic Kelly, 1846- . Title and publisher varies. 1846 issue reprinted Kings Lynn: Michael Winton, 1994. Covers parts of N.W. Kent.

Kelly's London suburban directory for 1894: southern suburbs. Kelly & Co., 1894. Includes N.W. Kent (now S.E. London)

Ashford

The Kent County Examiner directory of Ashford and popular calendar for 1896. Ashford: B.P. Boorman, 1896-1929.

Kentish Express guide and directory to Ashford, Romney Marsh, Tenterden, & district, including 80 towns & villages. Ashford: Kentish Express Office, 1911-35. Almost annual; title varies.

Headleys' directory of Ashford & District, including Willesborough, Kennington, Wye, Chilham, Charing, Lenham, Headcorn, Tenterden, Lydd, New Romney, Dymchurch, Sellindge, etc., etc. 2nd ed. Ashford: Headley Brothers, 1933.

Beckenham

Kelly's directory of Beckenham, Penge and Anerley. Kelly's directories, 1888-1938. 43 issues. Title varies.

Bexley

Local directory for Old Bexley, Bexleyheath, East Wickham, Welling, Barnehyrst, 1929. Bexleyheath: Bexley and District Publications, 1929.

Blackheath

The Blackheath, Lee and Lewisham directory for 1879-80. Blackheath: Ebenezer Wilmshurst, 1879.

The Blackheath, Lee, Lewisham and Greenwich directory ... Hutchings & Crowsley, 1883-6. 4 issues. Continued as *Kelly's Blackheath, Lee, Lewisham & Greenwich directory.* Kelly & Co., 1888-1938. Annual. Title varies.

Bromley

The Bromley directory. 5 issues. Bromley: E. Strong, 1866-1905. Merged with: *Kelly's Bromley directory (buff book), (with which is amalgamated Strong's Bromley directory).* Kelly's Directories, 1888-1960. Many issues; title varies.

Bush's Bromley budget and almanack, with directory of Bromley ... Bromley: S. Bush & Son, 1892-1914. Annual. Title varies.

Canterbury

Stapleton & Co's., topographical history and directory of Canterbury, Faversham, Herne-Bay, Sittingbourne, Whitstable ... Stapleton & Co., 1838. Re-published on 3 fiche, Maidstone: Kent County Council, [199-?]

MARTEN, CHARLES. *A directory for the City of Canterbury and its suburbs ...* Canterbury: Charles Marten, 1855. Also 1859 edition. The 1855 edition has been re-published on 1 fiche, Maidstone: Kent County Council, [199-?].

Green's Canterbury directory & court guide, including almanack for 1868. Brighton: Green and Co., [1867].

Directory of Canterbury and neighbourhood, with Faversham, Whitstable, Herne Bay, and all villages within a circuit of six miles from Canterbury ... 2 issues. Geo. Stevens, 1882-9. The 1889 edition has been re-published on 6 fiche, Maidstone: Kent County Council, [199-?].

Kelly's directory of Canterbury, Whitstable and Herne Bay, &c. Kelly & Co., 1890-1970. Many issues; title varies.

Pike's Canterbury & District, Herne Bay & Whitstable blue book and local directory for 18--. Brighton: Robinson Son & Pike, 1893-1939. Annual. Title and publisher varies; became *The Canterbury and district, Herne Bay & Whitstable local directory.*

Chatham

Fordham's Kentish advertiser, weather almanack and Chatham directory for the year 1842. Chatham: A.T. Fordham, 1841. Brief.

The monthly official Chatham directory, including Gravesend, Sheerness, and Shoeburyness. Chatham: Woolley & Co., 1895- 1914.

Chislehurst

1883[-7]: The Chislehurst, Bickley, Sidcup, and Cray Valley directory, with almanack & diary, to which are added notes of local interest. Chislehurst: Lewis Wing, 1882-6. 2 issues.

The Deal, Walmer and Sandwich directory: street directory, almanack and diary ... Deal: T.F. Pain & Sons, 1882-1948. Title varies; cover title: *T.F. Pain's Deal, Walmer and Sandwich directory ...*

Dartford

Dartford &c. directory, giving a complete alphabetical list of all the principal inhabitants ... J. Williams, 1850. Original title page missing on copy seen.

Dover

Dover and Deal directory and guide ... Dover: J. Horn & R. Long, 1792.

Dover, Folkestone, etc., etc. street directory for 1871. W. Tomkies, [1871]

Sinnock Howard and Co's. comprehensive street, trades and professional directory and court guide for Dover, Folkestone, Sandgate & Hythe ... Sinnock, Howard & Co., 1875.

Pike's Dover blue book and local directory. Brighton: Robinson Son & Pike, 1887-1939. Annual; title and publisher varies.

Eltham

Turner & Robinson's directory and almanack ... Contents: Eltham, New Eltham, and Mottingham. Eltham: Turner & Robinson, 1885-1906. Continued by: *Eltham, New Eltham, Well Hall and Mottingham.* Eltham: H.C. Digby, 1907-15. Annual.

Faversham

The Faversham directory and year book of useful information, with almanack ... Faversham: James Higham, 1862-91. Publisher varies; 1882 edition reprinted in facsimile as *Faversham reprints* 2. Faversham: Faversham Society, 1988.

Faversham & district directory. Faversham: Voile & Roberson, 1926 & 1939.

Folkestone

Creed's almanack for 1873, containing a newly compiled complete directory to Folkestone and neighbourhood and a concise guide to the locality. Folkestone: C. Creed, 1873.

Pike's Folkestone, Hythe and Sandgate directory and local blue book. Brighton: J.M. Robinson & Son, 1887-1904. Annual. Title varies.

Kelly's directory Folkestone, Sandgate, Hythe, Cheriton, &c., ... Kelly's Directories, 1896-1949. Title varies; many issues.

Parsons' Folkestone and district directory and local year book for 1910. Folkestone: F.J. Parsons, 1910.

Forest Hill

Green & Co's., Forest Hill, Sydenham, and Upper Norwood directory & court guide, including Penge, Anerley, Lower Norwood, etc., etc. Green & Co., 1867.

Kelly's Forest Hill, Lower Sydenham and part of Brockley directory (buff book) ... Kelly's Directories, 1889-1908. Annual.

Gravesend

Hall's Gravesend and Milton directory and advertiser, 1853. Gravesend: T. Hall, 1853-89. Title varies; also includes Northfleet.

Greenwich

Green's court guide and commercial directory and gazetter: Greenwich, Blackheath, Deptford, Lewisham, New Cross, Lee, for 1874-5. Green and Co., 1874.

Herne Bay

Ridout & Flower's Herne Bay directory and year book ... for 1884. Herne Bay: Ridout and Flower, 1884-1903. There may be later issues not seen.

Herne Bay press directory, with diary and almanack ... Herne Bay: Herne Bay Press, 1894.

Isle of Sheppey

Parsons Isle of Sheppey local directory and guide. Hastings: F.J. Parsons, [1901?]

Cole's Isle of Sheppey directory, 1909. Sheerness: W.J. Cole, 1908.

Isle of Thanet

Isle of Thanet directory, giving a complete alphabetical list of all the principal inhabitants in the towns ... J. Williams, 1849.

Bear's postal directory for Margate, Ramsgate, St. Lawrence, Broadstairs, and St. Peter's, containing alphabetically the names of tenants, both private and commercial ... Ramsgate: J. Bear, 1869.

Gregory & Co's. postal directory for Margate, including Ramsgate, St. Lawrence, Broadstairs, Westgate-on-Sea, and St. Peter's ... T. Gregory & Co., 1878.

Grant's directory of the Isle of Thanet, including Margate, Ramsgate, Broadstairs, Westgate, Birchington, &c., &c. ... 1883-4. [ ]: Grant, 1883.

Directory and guide to the Isle of Thanet, with map, including articles on the geology and farming of the island ... 2 issues. Hutchings and Crowsley, 1883-4.

Kelly's directory of the Isle of Thanet, with guide ('buff book'). Kelly's Directories, 1883-1974. Many issues.

Lewisham

Kelly's Lewisham, Brockley and Catford directory (buff book) ... Kelly & Co., 1899-1928. Annual.

Maidstone

PHIPPEN, JAMES. *New and enlarged directory for Maidstone and its environs ...* Maidstone: W. West, 1850. Includes 48 surrounding parishes.

[Maidstone, Canterbury, Dover & Tunbridge Wells directory & court guide, 1865-6.] [ ], 1866. Reprinted on 3 fiche. Maidstone: Kent County Library, [199-]. Title page missing on copy microfilmed.

The handy directory and guide for Maidstone and the surrounding villages, within a circle of six miles. Maidstone: W.S. Vivish, 1872.

Directory of Maidstone and neighbourhood, with East and West Malling, including all villages within a circuit of six miles from Maidstone ... Geo. Stevens, 1882-95. 5 issues.

The Kent Messenger directory of Maidstone and surrounding villages ... Maidstone: Kent Messenger, 1898-1938. 27 issues. Continued by *Kelly's ... directory of Maidstone and neighbourhood.* Kelly's Directories, 1947- .

Maidstone, Tunbridge Wells and Dover district trades directory ... 1904-5. Edinburgh: Town and County Directories, [1904].

Maidstone, Royal Tunbridge Wells, Dover, and South Kent district trades directory ... 1914-15. Manchester: Town and County Directories, 1914-32. 5 issues.

Penge

The Penge, Sydenham, Forest Hill & Norwood directory 1867-8. Penge: W. Aspinall, 1867.

Rochester

Kelly's directory of Rochester, Strood, Chatham, &c ... Kelly & Co., 1890-1974. Title varies.

Sevenoaks

Salmon's directory of Sevenoaks and neighbourhood. Sevenoaks: J. Salmon, 1914.

Sidcup

Sidcup directory ..., including Foots Cray and Lamorbey, with almanack and diary and all local information. Sidcup. C Forwood, 1905-7. 3 issues.

Sydenham

Clark's Sydenham and Forest Hill directory for 1859. Upper Sydenham: W.T. Clark, 1859.

Burt's Sydenham & Forest Hill guide and directory for 1862. Sydenham: Robert K. Burt, 1862.

Platt & Burdett's Sydenham, Forest Hill, and Penge directory for 1882, containing map of the Crystal Palace district, complete street arrangement, and alphabetical list of commercial and private residents ... Norwood: Platt & Burdett, 1880-82. 2 issues.

The Sydenham & Norwood directory. Hutchings & Crowley, 1882-6. Continued as: *Kelly's Sydenham, Norwood & Streatham directory (buff book).* Kelly & Co., 1887-1939. Title varies; includes Forest Hill.

WILLIAMS, W. ALLON. *The Sydenham, Forest Hill & Catford directory 1894, comprising alphabetical lists of streets, residents and tradesmen, together with general local information and new map of district.* Forest Hill: Victoria Printing Works, 1893. Described as 2nd annual ed.

Tenterden

Thomson almanack and local directory. Tenterden: W. Thomson, 1889-1940. Annual; title varies. For Tenterden.

Tunbridge Wells

Mathieson's Tunbridge Wells and Tonbridge (including Southborough, Frant & Pembury directory for 1867-8. Tunbridge Wells: Richard Relton, 1867.

Kelly's directory of Tunbridge Wells, Southborough, Tonbridge, and villages in the neighbourhood. Kelly's Directories, 1889-1965. Many issues. Title varies.

Weald

W.T. Pike's district blue book, Weald of Kent and Romney Marsh directory, 1884-1885, with historical notes. Hastings: W.T. Pike, [1884]. Re-published on 6 fiche, Maidstone: Kent County Council, [199-?]

Westerham

Hooker's directory 1937. Westerham: Hooker Bros., 1937. Described as '72nd year of publication', but no others seen.

Woolwich

Kelly's Woolwich, Plumstead, Shooters Hill, and Charlton directory (buff book) ... Kelly's Directories, 1893-1923. Annual.

B. Maps and Place Names

The place-names appearing in genealogical sources are frequently minor names, sometimes no longer used. There are two directories which can be used to identify obscure places; these volumes also give the meanings of names:

GLOVER, JUDITH. *The place names of Kent.* B.T. Batsford, 1976.

WALLENBERG, J.K. *The place-names of Kent.* Uppsala: Appelbergs Boktryckeriaktiebolag, 1934.

In order to locate places on modern Ordnance Survey maps, you need:

POOLE, ERIC. *Index of all Kent place names on 1″ O.S. map. 1957-69.* 2 fiche. K.F.H.S.R.P. **1040.**) 1987.

The original 1″ Ordnance Survey maps has been reprinted in book form in:

The old series Ordnance Survey maps of England and Wales ... volume I: Kent, Essex, E.Sussex, and S.Suffolk. Lympne Castle: Harry Margary, 1975. Facsimile sheet maps are also available from the publisher David and Charles.

Innumerable maps and places are available in the various libraries and record offices of the county; many are listed in:

BERGESS, WYN. *Kent maps and plans in the libraries of Kent and the adjoining London boroughs: a finding list.* Library Association London and Home Counties Branch, 1992.

Maps at the Centre for Kentish Studies are also listed in:

K.A.O. catalogues: Catalogue of maps. 3 fiche. K.F.H.S.R.P. **771.** 1986.

For estate maps, see:

HULL, F., ed. Catalogue of estate maps 1590-1840 in Kent County Archives Office. Maidstone: Kent County Council, 1973. Searchroom copy, with annotations, filmed as K.F.H.S.R.P. **681.** 1986. (6 fiche). For supplement, see **682.** (2 fiche). See also K.F.H.S.R.P. **769-70.**

7. OFFICIAL LISTS OF NAMES

A. *General*

The bureaucratic methods of government frequently require the compilation of lists of names. A variety of purposes are served by these lists — taxation, voting, land ownership, *etc*. They are invaluable sources of information for genealogists, and are essential for tracing the homes of family names. The earliest listing is Domesday book. A convenient modern edition is available:

MORGAN, PHILIP. ed. *Domesday book, 1: Kent*. Chichester: Phillimore, 1983.

B. *Taxation*

From the medieval period until the seventeenth century, the subsidy constituted an important source of government revenue. Each time it was levied, returns of those paying were compiled. A number of these returns have been printed, notably the 1334/5 return for the whole county:

HANLEY, H.A., & CHALKLIN, C.W., eds. 'The Kent lay subsidy of 1334/5', in DU BOULAY, F.R.H., eds. *Documents illustrative of medieval Kentish society*. Kent records **18**, 1964, 58-172 & 299-357.

A number of minor early tax lists for the whole county are also available:

GREENSTREET, JAMES, ed. 'Assessments in Kent for the aid to knight the Black Prince, anno 20 Edward III', *A.C.* **10**, 1876, 99-162.

GREENSTREET, JAMES. 'Kent contributors to a loan to the King, A.D. 1542', *A.C.* **11**, 1877, 398-404. 262 names.

'Subscribers towards the defence of the Realm, 1588', *K.F.H.S.J.* **1**(5), 1975, 96-8. List for Kent.

These are the only county-wide tax assessments in print. Reference may also, however, be made to the list of land tax assessments held at the Centre for Kentish Studies. These provide detailed listings of land owners and occupiers from the eighteenth century onwards. The list of assessments has been published on microfiche:

K.A.O. catalogues: T.C. (Commissioner of Taxes, including land tax); E.K.Y. (East Kent Yeomanry) W.K.R. (West Kent Regt.)

2 fiche. K.F.H.S.R.P. **766**. 1986. Also includes numerous miscellaneous documents relating to regimental history. Although there are no other county-wide assessments in print, many assessments for particular places have been published; these are available not just for the subsidy and land taxes, but also for hearth, window and poll taxes, *etc*. These are listed here by place.

Ash

FOX, PAUL A. 'The inhabitants of Ash-next-Sandwich in 1705: an index', *K.F.H.S.J.* **6**(11) 1992, 370-74. Index to land tax and bachelor tax returns, 1705.

Bexley

MANDY, W.H. 'A Bexley subsidy roll of A.D. 1301', *W.D.A.S.A.R.* **23**, 1926, 30-34.

Birchington

'Birchington land tax assessment 1719', *K.F.H.S.J.* **6**(2), 1990, 53-5. Transcript.

Blackheath

KIRBY, J.W., ed. *The royal subsidy of 1641 and the levy of 1644 on the inhabitants of Blackheath, Kent* ... published as *T.G.L.A.S.* **6**. 1963.

Bromley

WHYLER, FRED. 'Bromley: window and land tax, 1771', *N.W.K.F.H.* **3**(3), 1983, 95-7. Transcript.

Charlton

See Woolwich

Chelsfield

WHYLER, FRED. 'Chelsfield: land and window taxes, 1771', *N.W.K.F.H.* **2**(2), 1981, 52. Index of names.

Chislehurst

'Chislehurst, 1766 and 1767', *N.W.K.F.H.* **3**(12), 1985, 424- 5. Index to the window tax returns 1766, and the land tax return 1767.

Dartford

COATES, R.P. 'Valuation of the town of Dartford, 29 Ed. I', *A.C.* **9**, 1874, 285-98. Subsidy return, 1300-1301.

Deal
Land tax assessment for the town of Deal, Kent, [26] May 1726. 1 fiche. K.F.H.S.R.P. **169**. 1985.

Downe
'Downe residents, 1766', *N.W.K.F.H.* **2**(4), 1981, 144. List, presumably from Window Tax assessment.

Eltham
See Woolwich

Eynsford
DUNCOMBE, W.G., ed. *The hearth tax returns for Eynsford, Lullingstone & Farningham 1662-1671.* Publications **1**. [Farningham]: Farningham & Eynsford Local History Society, 1990.

Farnborough
WHYLER, FRED. 'Farnborough (Kent) residents, 1766 & 1767', *N.W.K.F.H.* **2**(6), 1992, 198. List, presumably from window tax assessments.

Farningham
See Eynsford

Faversham Hundred
GREENSTREET, JAMES. 'Subsidy roll for the Hundred of Faversham, A° 14 Henry VIII', *A.C.* **12**, 1878, 420-7. 1522-3.

Goudhurst
HILL, R.H. ERNEST. 'Mss. relating to Goudhurst and neighbourhood', *A.C.* **28**, 1909, 10-21. Includes wills of two John Horsmondens, 1526 and 1578, deed abstracts, 15-18th c., lay subsidies, 1642, *etc.*

Gravesend
GREEN, E.R., ed. *Hearth tax returns 1664: Gravesend, Milton, Northfleet and Southfleet.* Gravesend: privately published, 1984.

Hayes
WYLER, FRED. 'Hayes (Kent) landowners and residents 1766, 1767 & 1794', *N.W.K.F.H.* **2**(4), 1981, 162. See also 3(7), 1984, 239. List, presumably from land tax assessments.

Lewisham
COULTER, JOHN. 'Lewisham and the 1664 hearth tax returns', *T.G.L.A.S.* **10**(3), 1987, 119-27. Attempts identification of people with places.

Lullingstone
See Eynsford

Meopham
CARLEY, JAMES. 'Tudor taxes in Meopham', *B.K.* **6**(8), 1985, 468-70. Subsidy list for 1524.

Milton next Gravesend
See Gravesend

Northfleet
See Gravesend

Orpington
WHYLER, FRED. 'Orpington land taxes 1767', *N.W.K.F.H.* **7**(4), 1995, 124. Facsimile of assessment.
'Orpington residents, 1767', *N.W.K.F.H.* **2**(7), 1982, 240. Index to land tax return.

Ripple
'1816 land tax assessment for Ripple in Kent', *Manchester genealogist* **4**(1), 1968, 10.

Rochester
ARNOLD, A.A. 'The poll tax in Rochester, September 1660', *A.C.* **30**, 1914, 1-33. Includes transcript.

Saint Augustine's Lathe
HARRINGTON, DUNCAN W., ed. *Kent hearth tax enrolled assessment, 1664: lathe of St. Augustine. Kent Archives Office, Q/RTh.* K.F.H.S.R.P. **14**. 1983. Also available on 2 fiche.

Saint Mary Cray
WHYLER, FRED. 'St. Mary Cray, 1766/7', *N.W.K.F.H.* **2**(8), 1982, 278. Index to tax returns (presumably land tax?)

Saint Pauls Cray
'St. Pauls Cray, 1765 and 1786', *N.W.K.F.H.* **2**(4), 1981, 131. Index to land tax assessments.

Shepway Lathe
HARRINGTON, DUNCAN W., ed. *Hearth tax
enrolled asessment, 1664: Lathe of
Shepway, Kent.* 1 fiche. K.F.H.S.R.P. **182**.
1985.

Sittingbourne
RAWSON, MAUREEN. 'Sittingbourne land tax',
K.F.H.S.J. **7**(8) 1994, 276-7. List of land
tax payers, 1780.

Somerden Hundred
DURTNELL, C.S. 'The lay subsidy roll for
Somerden Hundred, 1327-8', *A.C.* **80**, 1965,
250-52.

Southfleet
See Gravesend

Speldhurst
STEBBING, W.P.D. 'The hearth tax for
Speldhurst in 1663', *A.C.* **48**, 1936, 251-3.

Woolwich
VINCENT, W.T. 'Our ancestors', *W.D.A.S.A.R.*
19, 1914, 50- 54. Includes the subsidies of
1542, 1570 and 1611, and the hearth tax,
1663, for Woolwich, Charlton and Eltham.

C. *Loyalty Oaths*

From time to time, governments demand
oaths of loyalty from their subjects. The
resultant lists can be invaluable to the
genealogist. Unfortunately, for Kent, only
one such list is in print, for only one parish.
The solemn league and covenant was an oath
taken in support of Parliament during the
Great Rebellion:
*Birchington solemn league and covenant
1643.* 1 fiche. K.F.H.S.R.P. **851**. 1986.
Filmed from the original manuscript.

D. *Poll Books*

In the eighteenth and nineteenth centuries,
voting was not secret, and poll books giving
the names of electors and how they cast
their votes were published after elections.
Many Kent pollbooks survive, although only
a handful of copies for each issue. Full lists
are given in the works listed in section 12D
of Raymond's *English genealogy: a
bibliography.* These supersede a much older
Kentish list, printed as:

MERCER, W.J. 'Poll books', *Notes and queries*
8, 1907, 177.
Many Kent pollbooks have been filmed for
the Kent Family History Society's record
publications. These are readily available on
fiche (almost all filmed from printed
volumes) and include:

Kent
*The poll for the knights of the shire to
represent the County of Kent in the year
1734.* 3 fiche. K.F.H.S.R.P. **184**. 1985.
*The poll for the knights of the shire to
represent the County of Kent in the year
1754.* 3 fiche. K.F.H.S.R.P. **185**. 1985.
*The poll for the knights of the shire to
represent the County of Kent in the year
1790.* 3 fiche. K.F.H.S.R.P. **186**. 1985.
*The poll for the knights of the shire to
represent the County of Kent in the year
1802.* 3 fiche. K.F.H.S.R.P. **187**. 1985.

East Kent
*The poll for the knights of the shire to
represent the Eastern Division of the
County of Kent in the year 1832 & 1852;
The poll of the electors for members of
Parliament to represent the City of
Canterbury in the year 1818, 1830 & 1832.*
6 fiche. K.F.H.S.R.P. **193**. 1985.
*The poll for the knights of the shire to
represent the Eastern Division of the
County of Kent in the year 1837.* 2 fiche.
K.F.H.S.R.P. **192**. 1985.
*The poll for the knights of the shire to
represent the Eastern Division of the
County of Kent in the year 1857.* 2 fiche.
K.F.H.S.R.P. **188**. 1985.
*The poll for the knights of the Shire to
represent the Eastern Division of the
County of Kent in the year 1863.* 2 fiche.
K.F.H.S.R.P. **189**. 1985.
*The poll for the knights of the shire to
represent the Eastern Division of the
County of Kent in the year 1865.* 3 fiche.
K.F.H.S.R.P. **190**. 1985.
*The poll for the knights of the shire to
represent the Eastern Division of the
County of Kent in the year 1868.* 8 fiche.
K.F.H.S.R.P. **191**. 1985.

West Kent
*1835 poll book for the Western Division of
the County of Kent.* 2 fiche. K.F.H.S.R.P.
41. 1985.

West Kent poll book, 1837. 3 fiche.
K.F.H.S.R.P. **776**. 1986.
*1847 poll book for the Western Division of
the County of Kent.* 2 fiche. K.F.H.S.R.P.
48. 1985.
West Kent poll book April 1852. 3 fiche.
K.F.H.S.R.P. **778**. 1986.
West Kent poll book July 1852. 3 fiche.
K.F.H.S.R.P. **777**. 1986.
West Kent poll book May 1859. 3 fiche.
K.F.H.S.R.P. **779**. 1986.
West Kent poll book July 1865. 5 fiche.
K.F.H.S.R.P. **780**. 1986.
West Kent poll book November 1868. 3 fiche.
K.F.H.S.R.P. **781**. 1986.

Canterbury
*Canterbury poll book, 1768: Cathedral
Archives and Library additional
manuscript number 29.* 1 fiche.
K.F.H.S.R.P. **157**. 1985. From the original
manuscript.
*The poll of the electors for Member of
Parliament to represent the City of
Canterbury in the County of Kent, in the
year 1780.* 1 fiche. K.F.H.S.R.P. **194**. 1985.
*Canterbury borough poll books for the years
1790 and 1796, bound together with
Cyprian Rondean Bunce, 'Citizen' pseud.,
A translation of the several charters
granted by Edward IV ... to the citizens of
Canterbury; also a list of the bailiffs and
mayors from the year 780 ... with a
description of the boundaries of the city
(1791).* 5 fiche. K.F.H.S.R.P. **158**. 1985.
*The poll of the electors for members of
Parliament to represent the City of
Canterbury in the County of Kent in the
year 1790.* 2 fiche. K.F.H.S.R.P. **195**. 1985.
*The poll of the electors for Members of
Parliament to represent the City of
Canterbury in the County of Kent in the
year 1835.* 1 fiche. K.F.H.S.R.P. **196**. 1985.
*The poll of the electors for Members of
Parliament to represent the City of
Canterbury in the County of Kent in the
year 1837.* 1 fiche. K.F.H.S.R.P. **197**. 1985.
*The poll of the electors for Members of
Parliament to represent the City of
Canterbury in the county of Kent in the
year 1837, 1841, 1857, 1865, 1868.* 3 fiche.
K.F.H.S.R.P. **198**. 1985.

*The poll of the electors for Members of
Parliament to represent the City of
Canterbury in the County of Kent in the
year June 1841.* 1 fiche. K.F.H.S.R.P. **199**.
1985.
*The poll of the electors for Members of
Parliament to represent the City of
Canterbury in the County of Kent in the
year 1847.* K.F.H.S.R.P. **200**. 1985.
*The poll of the electors for Members of
Parliament to represent the city of
Canterbury in the County of Kent in the
year 1852.* 1 fiche. K.F.H.S.R.P. **201**. 1985.
*The poll of the electors for Members of
Parliament to represent the City of
Canterbury in the County of Kent in the
year 1854.* 1 fiche. K.F.H.S.R.P. **202**. 1985.
*The poll of the electors for Members of
Parliament to represent the City of
Canterbury in the County of Kent in the
year 1862.* 1 fiche. K.F.H.S.R.P. **203**. 1985.
For the 1818, 1830 and 1832 polls, see under
East Kent, above.

Dover
*Dover register of electors 1802 and
monumental inscriptions of St. Martins
burial ground.* 1 fiche. K.F.H.S.R.P. **1520**.
[199- ?].
*The poll for two barons to serve in
Parliament for the town and port of
Dover, Kent, June 1826.* 1 fiche.
K.F.H.S.R.P. **206**. 1985.

Maidstone
*Maidstone ward lists, Oct. 1859, Oct. 1861,
Oct. 1864, Nov. 1868 & October 1870.* 3
fiche. K.F.H.S.R.P. **1686**. 1992. Not seen.

E. *Census Returns*

The census returns of the nineteenth century
are much used by genealogists, and a variety
of indexes have been compiled. For a
detailed guide to those available for Kent,
1801-1891, consult:
RICKARD, GILLIAN. *Kent census surname
index.* 4th ed. Canterbury: the author, 1997.

i. *Early Returns*
Surviving census returns are normally
available every ten years from 1841. However,
a number of earlier returns do survive, as
do a few private censuses. Many are listed in:

BOURNE, SUSAN. *Early census returns for Kent, 1801-1831: a practical guide for the family historian.* Aylesford: Prospect Litho, 1996.
Some of these early returns have been printed, and are listed here by parish.

Beckenham
'The 1821 census of Beckenham', *N.W.K.F.H.* 1(6), 1980, 164- 6. Index.

Bromley
'The 1801 census of Bromley', *N.W.K.F.H.* 1(5), 1980, 128- 31. Index to heads of households.

Deal
St. Leonard, Deal: original returns for the census returns of 1801, 1811 and 1821. 6 fiche. K.F.H.S.R.P. **177.** 1985. From the original manuscripts.

Hayes
SILVERTHORNE, ELIZABETH. 'Hayes parish census 1790', *N.W.K.F.H.* 4(4), 1986, 132-5. List of 58 households.

Stansted
DOBSON, MARY J. 'Original Compton census returns: the Shoreham Deanery', *A.C.* **94,** 1979, 61-73. Includes lists of the inhabitants of Wrotham and Stansted, 1676.
MEADEN, LINDA. 'The Compton census 1676', *N.W.K.F.H.* 2(7), 1982, 235-6. One of the few surviving lists of names from this census, for Stansted, Kent.

Wrotham
See Stansted

ii. *General*
Census indexes 1841 to 1881. K.F.H.S.R.P. 834-48. 1986. Contents:
  834. River and Poulton. 6 fiche.
  835. Whitfield. 3 fiche.
  836. Guston. 3 fiche.
  837. St. Margarets at Cliffe. 8 fiche.
  838. Westcliffe. 2 fiche.
  839. Oxney. 1 fiche.
  840. East Langdon. 4 fiche.
  841. West Langdon. 2 fiche.
  842. Langdon strays. 1 fiche.
  843. Ashley, Northbourne. 2 fiche.
  844. Ripple. 3 fiche.
  845. Ringwould. 5 fiche.
  846. Kingsdown. 4 fiche.
  847. Sutton, Dover. 3 fiche.
  848. Sholden. 5 fiche.

iii. *1841*

Charlton
'Charlton census for 1841', *W.D.F.H.S.J.* **3,** 1980, 3-5. Surname list only.

Greenwich
'Surname index for the 1841 Greenwich census', *W.D.F.H.S.J.* **36,** 1989, 16-23; **37,** 1990, 20-26; **38,** 1990, 14-19; **39,** 1990, 20-24; **40,** 1990, 20-24; **42,** 1991, 18-21; **43,** 1991, 20-23; **44,** 1991, 27-32; **45,** 1992, 31-6; **46,** 1992, 36-9.

Milton next Sittingbourne
1841 census index for Milton Registration District. Fiche. K.F.H.S.R.P. **1707.** 1995. Not seen.

Woolwich
'Woolwich census for 1841', *W.D.F.H.S.J.* **4,** 1980, 7-10; **5,** 1981, 9-12; **6,** 1981, 2-6; **15,** 1983, 12-15; **19,** 1984, 17-18; **20,** 1984, 25-7; **21,** 1985, 24-5; **22,** 1985, 23-5; **24,** 1985, 18- 28.

iv. *1851*
COPUS, MATTHEW. '1851 census indexes for Kent, Sussex and Surrey', *K.F.H.S.J.* 4(12), 1986, 437-9. Discussion of various indexes.

Ashford
RUDERMAN, ARTHUR. *Index to 1851 census of Ashford.* 1 fiche. K.F.H.S.R.P. **1525.** 1989.

Bromley
1851 census index for North West Kent. 5 vols. [ ]: North West Kent Family History Society, 1988-93. v.1 Bromley Registration District. v.2. Woolwich parish. v.3. Deptford, St. Paul & St. Nicholas Parishes. v.4. Lewisham R.D. v.5. Dartford R.D.

Canterbury
PARRY, COLIN J. 'Missing from home!', *K.F.H.S.J.* 1(7) 1986, 138-44. Extracts from the 1851 census of Canterbury for almshouses, hospitals, schools, the workhouse, *etc.*

Cheriton

'1851 census, Cheriton, Folkestone: Shorncliffe Barracks, Convict Station', *K.C.* 4(7), 1987, 191-4; 4(8), 1987, 206-9.

Chilham

Chilham 1851 census returns & P.Rs.: marriages 1800-1851. 2 fiche. K.F.H.S.R.P. 1663. 1992.

Dartford

See Bromley

Deptford

See Bromley

Dover

WEBSTER, MARTYN C. *Alphabetical index to the 1851 census for Dover, Kent, H.O. 107 1632.* 6 fiche. [Brighton]: M.C. Webster, 1993. This covers the Dover area, but not the central parishes of St. Mary and St. James.

Greenwich

KEYMER, E.W.L. *1851 census surname index, East and West Greenwich Registration Districts.* 1 fiche. [E.W.L. Keymer?], 1992.
KEYMER, E.W.L. 'Indexers and their indexes: Greenwich in 1851', *Family tree magazine* 9(2), 1992, 42. Description of a census index available on fiche.

Isle of Sheppey

PENNEY, COLIN. 'Sheppey census transcriptions', *K.F.H.S.J.* 6(5), 1990, 161. Lists policemen in the 1851 census.
PENNEY, COLIN. 'Sheppey census transcription', *K.F.H.S.J.* 6(6), 1991, 194-5. Lists clergy and coastguards in the 1851 census.
PENNEY, COLIN. 'Sheppey census transcriptions', *K.F.H.S.J.* 6(7), 1991, 236-7. List of miscellaneous occupations from the 1851 census.
PENNEY, COLIN. 'Sheppey census transcriptions', *K.F.H.S.J.* 6(12), 1992, 417-20. Lists entries for various occupations 1851 and 1881.

Isle of Thanet

SWINFIELD, G.M. *The 1851 census index of Kent.* [Canterbury]: Institute of Heraldry & Genealogical Studies, 1984. Vol. 1. Thanet Registration District.

Lee

BIRCHENOUGH, JOSEPHINE. 'A census-taker's eye view of Lee in 1851', *N.W.K.F.H.* 3(6), 1984, 199-201.

Lewisham

WAGHORN, LEN. 'Lewisham Workhouse', *N.W.K.F.H.* 3(8), 1984, 271-3. Includes list of surnames from the 1851 census.
See also Bromley

Minster in Sheppey

PENNEY, COLIN. '1851 census, union workhouse, Minster, Sheppey', *K.F.H.S.J.* 5(3), 1987, 98-100.
PENNEY, COLIN. '1851 census parish union: Minster, Isle of Sheppey (the Workhouse) HO 107.1628', *K.F.H.S.J.* 5(7), 1988, 264-6. Transcript.

New Romney

'1851 census: New Romney Workhouse', *K.C.* 4(3), 1986, 72-4.

Tonbridge

GOWIN, W. 'Out-strays: 1851-81 census returns, Tonbridge, Kent', *W.D.F.H.S.J.* 31, 1988, 18-20.

Woolwich

See Bromley

Out of County

HARNDEN, JOHN. 'Strays from the 1851 census for Herefordshire, reel no. HO 107 1978', *K.F.H.S.J.* 5(1), 1986, 25; 5(5), 1987, 180-81. Kentish inhabitants of Herefordshire.

v.1871

Stone

St. Mary's Female Penitentiary, Stone, Dartford. 1 fiche. N.W.K.F.H.S., 1996. Transcript and index of censuses, 1871, 1881 and 1891.

Out of County

DAVIES, COLIN. 'Kent orphans', *K.F.H.S.J.* 7(1), 1992, 26-7. 1871 and 1881 census of the New Orphanage, Ashley Down Road, Horfield, Glos., relating to Kentish children.

vi. 1881

1881 census surname index: Kent. 132 fiche. Church of Jesus Christ of Latter Day Saints, 1990. Important.

Isle of Thanet
NORWOOD, PETER. 'Isle of Thanet census, 1881', *Suffolk roots: the journal of the Suffolk Genealogy Society* 10(4), 1984, 95-6; 12(1), 1986, 14-15; 12(3), 1986, 70-72. Many names.

Woolwich
BONWELL, LES. 'Norfolk strays from Woolwich census, 1881: district of Holy Trinity, Kent', *Norfolk ancestor: journal of the Norfolk and Norwich Genealogical Society* 4(5), 1986, 78.

'1881 census (RG10/775-778) for Woolwich Barracks, Kent: extracts of soldiers born in Suffolk', *Suffolk roots: the journal of the Suffolk Genealogy Society* 14(3), 1988, 82.

Out of County
NICOL, RUTH. 'Kent men found in Guernsey 1881 census', *K.F.H.S.J.* 8(4), 1996, 149.

TRICKETT, F. 'Kent strays in Hampshire: 1881 census, Royal Navy Hospital, Haslar, Alverstoke', *K.F.H.S.J.* 6(9), 1991. 308.

BOWYER, J. 'Kent strays from 1881 census of Mile End Old Town, Middlesex', *K.F.H.S.J.* 8(4), 1996, 151; 8(5), 1996, 221.

EDGE, JOAN M.T. 'Kent strays from 1881 census Middlesex: Bromley St. Leonard, Poplar (St. Michael and All Angels) RG11/0502 folio 33', *K.F.H.S.J.* 8(5), 1996, 222-3.

BRENCHLEY, A.G. 'Kent strays found in Northamptonshire 1881 census', *K.F.H.S.J.* 6(9), 1991, 302-3.

vii.1891

Brenchley
VALE, JO. 'List of 'strays', lodging in the Horsmonden district of Brenchley, Kent, on the night of 8 April 1891', *W.F.H.S.J.* 5, 1994, 16. From the census.

Milton next Sittingbourne
1891 census index: Milton Registration District. Fiche. K.F.H.S.R.P. 1768. 1996. Not seen

Out of County
DAVIES, COLIN. 'Kent born orphans 1891 in the Müller Homes (New Orphanage), Ashley Down Road, Horfield', *K.F.H.S.J.* 8(4), 1996, 150-51. In Gloucestershire.

STANLEY, ROSEMARY. 'Kent strays from 1891 census of Portsmouth', *K.F.H.S.J.* 8(5), 1996, 224; 8(6), 1997, 278- 9.

E. Landowners

A different type of census was taken in 1873. Everyone who owned an acre or more of land was listed, and the returns were published in the Parliamentary Papers. See: 'Kent', in *Return of owners of land 1873, vol.I.* House of Commons Parliamentary paper, 1874, LXXII, pt.1, 559-610. There is a 19th century reprint of this census: *The Domesday book for the County of Kent, being that portion of a return of owners of land ... in the year 1873 which refers to the county of Kent ...* Lewes: Sussex Express Office, 1877.

F. Tithe Maps and Apportionments

The Tithe Commutation Act of 1836 produced a vast collection of tithe maps and apportionments, now held in the Public Record Office and in many local record offices. Tithe apportionments list all land owners and occupiers, and are consequently invaluable sources for locating ancestors. Those held in the Centre for Kentish Studies are listed in:

K.A.O. catalogues: List of tithe maps and awards. 1 fiche. K.F.H.S.R.P. 767. 1986.

K.A.O. catalogues: Tithe maps, awards & altered apportionments C.T.R. & C.T.S. 4 fiche. K.F.H.S.R.P. 768. 1986.

Canterbury Archives and Library, Canterbury. To/A-W Canterbury Diocesan tithe records ... 3 fiche. K.F.H.S.R.P. 960. [1981?]

A number of tithe maps and apportionments etc., have been filmed for the Kent Family History Society's record publication; these include:

Acol
Acol altered tithe apportionment award and map, 1926. 5 fiche. K.F.H.S.R.P. 548. 1986.

Acol tithe redemption certificates, 20th c. 2
fiche. K.F.H.S.R.P. **546.** 1986.

Birchington
*All Saints, Birchington tithe altered
  apportionments ...* 18 + 2 fiche.
  K.F.H.S.R.P. **542-3.** 1986. Filmed from the
  original manuscripts.
*All Saints, Birchington tithe certs. of
  redemption & rent charge 1891-1936.* 3
  fiche. K.F.H.S.R.P. **544.** 1986. Filmed from
  the original manuscripts.
*All Saints, Birchington tithe redemption
  certs., 1895-1932.* 17 fiche. K.F.H.S.R.P.
  547. 1986.
Birchington & Acol tithe accts., 1899-1911
  1 fiche. K.F.H.S.R.P. 1986. Filmed from the
  original accounts.
*Birchington altered apportionments and
  map, 8 Jne 1886.* 2 fiche. K.F.H.S.R.P. **850.**
  1986.

Chilham
*Chilham: tithe apportionment & Chilham
  Castle estate.* 3 fiche. K.F.H.S.R.P. **1664.**
  1992. Index, etc.

Deal
Deal tithe map and apportionment. 3 fiche.
  K.F.H.S.R.P. **744.** 1986. 1843.

Elham
*Elham, Kent, tithe account book for the
  years 1784-1801.* 3 fiche. K.F.H.S.R.P. **309.**
  1986. Filmed from the original
  manuscript.

Sibertswold
*Shepherdswell, Kent: tithe apportionment
  records, 1841-1949.* 4 fiche. K.F.H.S.R.P.
  341. 1986. Filmed from the original
  records.

Sturry
*Sturry, Kent: redemption of tithe rate
  charges 1905-1932 ... & notes of epitaphs.* 2
  fiche. K.F.H.S.R.P. **273.** 1986. Filmed from
  the original manuscripts.

8. ESTATE PAPERS

A. General
The records of estate administration
constitute a mine of information for the
genealogist. Much is in print, although much
more lies untouched in the archives. Deeds,
surveys, accounts, etc., may all be made to
yield valuable genealogical information. For
a listing of medieval accounts held in various
repositories, see:
GALLOWAY, JAMES A., MURPHY, MARGARET,
  & MYHIL, OLWEN, etc. *Kentish demesne
  accounts up to 1350: a catalogue.* Centre
  for Metropolitan History, 1993.
Numerous estate documents and family
papers held at Kent Archives Office are
calendared in:
K.A.O. unofficial catalogues ... Fiche.
  F.F.H.S.R.P. **462-83 & 549-649.** 1986.
An antiquary's collection of deeds, many of
which are from Kent, is calendared in:
FAWTIER, ROBERT. 'Hand-lists of charters and
  deeds in the possession of the John
  Rylands Library', IV: the Phillips charters,
  *Bulletin of the John Rylands Library,
  Manchester.* **9,** 1925, 248-85. Lists
  numerous deeds from various places in
  Derbyshire, Yorkshire and Kent, and from
  Stilton, Huntingdonshire and Stainton
  with Streatham, Co. Durham, *etc.*
For calendars of a bookseller's collection of
Kent deeds, see:
'The value of old parchment deeds in
  genealogical and topographical research',
  Topographical quarterly, **2**(4), 1934, 293-
  334.
'Palaeography, genealogy and topography',
  Topographical quarterly **6**(3), 1938, 135-83.
A rental listing tenants in many parts of
Kent has been published on fiche:
*Rental of 'estates in possession', Kent: Lady
  Day, 1870.* 1 fiche. K.F.H.S.R.P. **176.** 1985.
  From the original manuscript, with typed
  index. It is not clear who the landowner
  was.
Sale catalogues are listed in:
*Sale catalogues of properties, stock and
  furniture 1894-1956.* 4 fiche. K.F.H.S.R.P.
  683. 1986. Reproduced from the original
  manuscript. This appears to be a listing of
  records at Kent Archives Office.

Insurance policy records are little used by genealogists, but are very useful for identifying policy holders. Many records have been filmed for Kent Family History Society's *record publications;* see: *Insurance policy book of Hedley Peters & Son.* 29 books on 147 fiche. K.F.H.S.R.P. **366-98.** 1986. Most books relate to particular insurance companies, e.g., the Royal Insurance Co., however three of these fiche deal with other subjects: **396.** Emigration records 1913-1949. **397.** Travel-emigration records 1945-1955. **398.** Sittingbourne registers, list of incumbents and churchwardens.

Feet of fines

The curiously named 'feet of fines' constitute a major source of evidence for tracing the descent of estates. They record innumerable land transactions from the medieval period to the nineteenth century. For a brief introduction, see:
HARRINGTON, KEN. 'Kent feet of fines', *K.F.H.S.J.* **5**(10), 1989, 381-2.
The medieval feet of fines for Kent have been calendared in a number of works:
CHURCHILL, IRENE J., GRIFFIN, RALPH, & HARDMAN, F.W. [eds.] *Calendar of Kent feet of fines to the end of Henry III's reign.* Kent records **15.** 1956. This supersedes:
L[ARKING], L.B. ed. 'Pedes finium', *A.C.* **1,** 1858, 217-88; **2,** 1859, 239-78; **3,** 1860; 209-40; **4,** 1861, 273-308; **5,** 1863, 259-90; **6,** 1866, 225-34. Covers 1195-1215.
GREENSTREET, JAMES. 'Abstracts of the Kent fines (pedes finium) levied in the reign of Edward II', *A.C.* **11,** 1877, 305-58; **12,** 1878, 289-308; **13,** 1880, 289-320; **14,** 1882, 241-80; **15,** 1883, 273-310.
GREENSTREET, JAMES. 'Abstracts of the feet of fines for Kent, temp Edward III', *A.C.* **18,** 1889, 337-52; **20,** 1893, 161- 86.
An edition of the Kent feet of fines edited by Michael Zell is due for publication in the Kent records series by Kent Archaeological Society..

Gavelkind

In order to understand Kent deeds, it may be useful to consult works on gavelkind — the peculiarly Kentish custom of inheritance.

These include:
ELTON, CHARLES I. *The tenures of Kent.* James Parker, 1867.
ROBINSON, THOMAS. *The common law of Kent, or, the customs of gavelkind, with the decisions concerning borough-English.* New ed. by J.D. Norwood. Ashford: Henry Igglesden, 1858.
SANDYS, CHARLES. *Consuetudines Kanciae: a history of gavelkind and other remarkable customs in the County of Kent.* John Russell Smith, 1851. Mentions names of many landowners.

Enclosure awards

Enclosure awards list the owners and tenants of the land to be enclosed. Those for Kent are listed in:
TATE, W.E. 'A hand-list of English enclosure acts and awards, part 17: open fields, commons and enclosures in Kent', *A.C.* **56,** 1944, 54-67.

B. *Family Papers*

Amherst
HULL, F. *Amherst mss.* 4 fiche. K.F.H.S.R.P. **473.** 1986. Lists estate papers from Kent, Essex and Surrey; also many personal papers.

Andrus
ANDRUS, F.S. 'Extracts from the miscellany and farm accounts of Francis Andrus of Scadbury in the parish of Southfleet', *A.C.* **100,** 1985, 371-83. Covers 1823-37; many names.

Bertie
CLARK, G.T. 'Original documents of the Berties of Bertiestead or Bersted', *Archaeological journal* **31,** 1874, 286-8. Medieval deeds, with notes on the descent of Bertie.

Brockman
BUTCHER, BURFORD. 'The Brockman papers', *A.C.* **43,** 1931, 281-3. Brief note on a collection of c.2000 deeds, 13-19th c., includes pedigree of Brockman, 16-19th c.
B., H.I. 'The Brockman charters', *British Museum quarterly* **6,** 1931-2, 75. Brief note on a large collection of Kent deeds.

Cobb
HULL, F. *Cobb mss.* 11 fiche. K.F.H.S.R.P.
476-7. 1986. Papers relating to a Margate
brewery; includes pedigree of Cobb, 18-
20th c.

Cobham
L[ARKING], L.B. 'Collectanea for a history of
the family of Cobham, with much of the
City of Rochester', *A.C.* **2**, 1859, 226-30.
Deeds, 13th c.

Cornwallis
See Mann

Cripps
*Catalogue of documents presented to the
Kent County Council by Major Sir
Frederick Cripps, D.S.O.* 2 fiche.
K.F.H.S.R.P. **774.** 1986. Calendar of Cripps
family estate papers *etc.*

Dalison
ROBERTSON, W.A. SCOTT. 'Dalison documents
from the muniment chests at Hamptons,
near Tunbridge, and a pedigree', *A.C.* **15**,
1883, 386-403. See also **16**, 1886, 64-5.
Includes rent rolls, 15th and 17th c.,
various medieval deeds, accounts, will and
executors accounts of Sir Maximilian
Dalyson, 1630, *etc.,* also pedigree,
16-19th c.

Dering
L[ARKING], L.B. 'On the Surrenden charters',
A.C. **1**, 1858, 50-65. Brief notes on Dering
muniments.

Dudley
See Sidney

Fitz Gilbert
MORTIMER, RICHARD. 'The beginnings of the
Honour of Clare', in BROWN, R. ALLEN, ed.
*Proceedings of the Battle Conference on
Anglo-Norman Studies* **3**, 1980, 119-41. 11th
c. estates of Richard Fitz Gilbert in
Suffolk, Kent, Surrey, Essex *etc.*
MORTIMER, RICHARD. 'Land and service: the
tenants of the Honour of Clare', *Anglo-
Norman studies: proceedings of the Battle
Conference* **8**, 1985, 177-97. Studies of
11-12th c. tenants in Suffolk, Kent, Surrey,
Essex, etc.

Hatton Wood
TAYLOR, F. 'The Hatton Wood manuscripts in
the John Rylands Library', *Bulletin of the
John Rylands Library* **24**, 1940, 357-75.
Brief description of a collection which,
although primarily of Cheshire interest,
does include charters from Kent,
Gloucestershire, *etc.*

Lisle
See Sidney

Mann
SHORROCKS, D.M.M. *Mann (Cornwallis) mss.*
2 fiche. K.F.H.S.R.P. **471.** 1986. Estate
papers relating to Linton, Egerton,
Cranbrook, *etc.*

Master
DALISON, MRS. 'Expense-book of James
Master, esq.', *A.C.* **15**, 1883, 160-216; **16**,
1886, 241-59; **17**, 1887, 321-52; **18**, 1889, 114-
68. 17th c. Includes a 'life'.

Romney
Romney of the Mote mss., 1461-1957. 4 + 4
fiche. K.F.H.S.R.P. **474-5.** 1986. Estate
papers relating to Maidstone, Westminster,
etc., especially rich for the 19th c.

Sackville
HISTORICAL MANUSCRIPTS COMMISSION.
*Calendar of the manuscripts of Major-
General Lord Sackville, K.B.E., C.B.E.,
C.M.G., preserved at Knole, Sevenoaks,
Kent.* 2 vols. H.M.S.O., 1940-66. Includes
pedigrees of Sackville, c.1520-1940, and
Cranfield and Randall, 1521-1617; primarily
lists the business papers of Lionel
Cranfield, 1551-1612.

Scott
'Receipts and expenditure of Sir John Scott,
in the reign of Edward IV', *A.C.* **10**, 1876,
250-8. Personal accounts.

Sidney
KINGSFORD, C.L., *et al,* eds. *Report on the
manuscripts of Lord De L'Isle and
Dudley preserved at Penshurst Place.* 6
vols. H.M.S.O., 1925-66. Sidney family
papers, relating to Penshurst, Tattershall,
Lincolnshire, *etc.* The estate papers are in
vol. 1.

HULL, F. *De L'Isle mss.* 12 fiche. K.F.H.S.R.P. **481-3.** 1986. Sidney family estate and family papers.

Stanhope
MILLS, MARIAN, ed. *Your most dutyfull servant: the correspondence between Grizel, Countess Stanhope of Chevening in Kent, and John Brampton, her steward, between the years 1764 and 1774.* Sevenoaks: Marian Mills, 1992.
Stanhope of Chevening mss. and related collections. 11 fiche. K.F.H.S.R.P. **478-80.** 1986.
Catalogue of the Stanhope of Chevening mss. Part 4. Index. K.A.O. U1590; U1000/4; U1384; U1450. 2 fiche K.F.H.S.R.P. **462.** 1986.

Toke
LODGE, ELEANOR C., ed. *The account book of a Kentish estate, 1616-1704.* Records of the social and economic history of England and Wales **6.** Oxford University Press, 1927. Account book of the Toke family of Godinton.

Tufton
HULL, FELIX, ed. 'The Tufton sequestration papers', in *A seventeenth century miscellany.* Kent records, **17,** 1960, 35- 67.

Twysden
Twysden & Twisden mss. 2 fiche. K.F.H.S.R.P. **472.** 1986. Of Goudhurst, Roydon, East Peckham, *etc.*
Catalogue of the Twysden and Twisden mss. [Maidstone]: Kent County Council, 1977. Includes diaries, letters, deeds, wills, etc., as well as official papers.

Wotton
F., R. 'A survey of the Wotton estate', *British Museum quarterly* **7,** 1932-3, 20-21. Brief note on a 16th c. survey and rental.

C. *Ecclesiastical Estates, etc.*

Archdiocese of Canterbury
SAYERS, JANE. *Estate documents of Lambeth Palace Library: a short catalogue.* [Leicester]: Leicester U.P., 1965. Mostly relates to Kent, Surrey and Sussex. Important.

CHURCHILL, IRENE JOSEPHINE, ed. *East Kent records: a calendar of some unpublished deeds and court rolls in the library of Lambeth Palace, with appendixes referring especially to the manors of Knowlton, Sandown, South Court, and North Court.* Kent records **7.** 1920-22.
HEAL, F. 'Archbishop Laud revisited: leases and estate management at Canterbury and, Winchester before the Civil War', in O'DAY, ROSEMARY & HEAL, FELICITY, eds. *Princes and paupers in the English church 1500-1800.* Leicester: Leicester University Press, 1981, 129-51. For background.

Bilsington Priory
NEILSON, N., ed. *The cartulary and terrier of the Priory of Bilsington, Kent.* Records of the social and economic history of England and Wales **7.** Oxford University Press, 1928.
WOODRUFF, C. EVELEIGH. 'Notes on some early documents relating to the manor, church and Priory of Bilsington, Kent', *A.C.* **41,** 1929, 1936. Abstracts of 18 deeds, 13-17th c.

Canterbury
DUNCOMBE, JOHN, & BATTELY, NICHOLAS. *The history and antiquities of the three archiepiscopal hospitals at and near Canterbury, viz., St. Nicholas, at Harbledown, St. Johns, Northgate, and St. Thomas, of Eastbridge, with some account of the Priory of St. Gregory, the Nunnery of St. Sepulchre, the Hospital of St. James and St. Lawrence, and Maynards Spittle.* J. Nichols, 1785. Includes many abstracts of deeds *etc.*

Canterbury. Cathedral
Many works relating to Canterbury Cathedral are available. Those relating to its estates are listed here; many others are cited in section 11 and elsewhere in this bibliography. Various lists and discussions of the Cathedral's muniments have been published:
'The muniments of the Dean and Chapter of Canterbury', in HISTORICAL MANUSCRIPTS COMMISSION. *Report on manuscripts in various collections, vol. 1.* Cd. 784. H.M.S.O., 1901, 205-81.

SHEPPARD, J. BRIGSTOCKE. 'Second report on historical manuscripts belonging to the Dean and Chapter of Canterbury', in HISTORICAL MANUSCRIPTS COMMISSION. *Eighth report ... Appendix, Part 1 (section II).* H.M.S.O., 1881, 315-55. Includes list of wills proved *sede vacante,* 1500-1501.

SHEPPARD, J. BRIGSTOCKE. 'Third report on historical mss. belonging to the Dean and Chapter of Canterbury', in HISTORICAL MANUSCRIPTS COMMISSION. *Ninth report ... Part 1. Report and appendix.* H.M.S.O., 1883, 72-129.

C.A.L.C. Catalogue: Christchurch Cathedral Priory & Christchurch altar endowment charters. 5 fiche. K.F.H.S.R.P. **962.** [198-?] Calendar of accounts, deeds, etc., medieval-19th c.

BOX, E.G. 'Donations of manors to Christ Church, Canterbury, and appropriation of churches', *A.C.* **44,** 1932, 103-19. Describes relevant archives.

Detailed editions and studies of particular documents include (in rough chronological order):

'Ee. v. 31', in *A catalogue of the manuscripts preserved in the library of the University of Cambridge.* vol.2. Cambridge: University Press, 1857, 190-250. Calendar of the register of Christ Church Priory, Canterbury, 12-14th c.

DOUGLAS, DAVID C., ed. *The Domesday monachorum of Christ Church, Canterbury.* Royal Historical Society, 1944. 11-12th c.

COLVIN, H.M. ed. 'A list of the Archbishop of Canterbury's tenants by Knight-service in the reign of Henry II', in DU BOULAY, F.R.H., ed. *Documents illustrative of medieval Kentish society.* Kent records **18.** 1964, 1-40. Includes many notes on tenants, 12th c.

BLORE, W.P. 'Recent discoveries in the archives of Canterbury Cathedral', *A.C.* **58,** 1946, 28-39. Accounts of the *carpentarius.*

BARNES, PATRICIA M. 'Documents concerning Christ Church Cathedral Priory, Canterbury, 1207-1213', in BARNES, PATRICIA M., & POWELL, W. RAYMOND, eds. *Interdict documents.* Pipe Roll Society 72; N.S., **34.** 1960, 33-104. Survey, naming tenants.

HALL, HUBERT, & NICHOLAS, FRIEDA J. 'Manorial accounts of the Priory of Canterbury, 1260-1420 (lists of beadles' rolls relating to twenty-two selected manors)', *Bulletin of the Institute of Historical Research* **8,** 1930-31, 137-55. Includes index of beadles.

HUSSEY, R.C. 'Documents from the archives of Christ Church, Canterbury', *A.C.* **10,** 1876, 316-9. Various accounts, etc., 15th c.

DU BOULAY, F.R.H. 'Calendar of the demesne leases made by Archbishop Warham (1503-32), excerpted from Dean and Chapter of Canterbury mss, register T', in DU BOULAY, F.R.H., ed. *Documents illustrative of medieval Kentish society.* Kent records **18,** 1964, 266-97.

WOODRUFF, C. EVELEIGH. 'A seventeenth-century survey of the estates of the Dean and Chapter of Canterbury in East Kent', *A.C.* **38,** 1926, 29-44.

Historical studies based on the Cathedral's muniments include:

SMITH, R.A.L. *Canterbury Cathedral Priory: a study in monastic administration.* Cambridge: Cambridge University Press, 1943. Scholarly; includes useful bibliography.

MATE, MAVIS. 'Agrarian economy after the Black Death: the manors of Canterbury Cathedral Priory 1348-91', *Economic history review* 2nd series **37,** 1984, 341-54. General study.

MATE, MAVIS. 'Property investment by Canterbury Cathedral Priory', *Journal of British Studies* **23**(2), 1984, 1-21. General study.

MATE, MAVIS. 'Coping with inflation: a fourteenth-century example', *Journal of medieval history* **4,** 1978, 95-107. Study of the accounts of Canterbury Cathedral Priory.

MATE, MAVIS. 'The farming out of manors: a new look at the evidence from Canterbury Cathedral Priory', *Journal of medieval history* **9,** 1983, 331-43.

MATE, MAVIS. 'The estates of Canterbury Priory before the Black Death 1315-1348', *Studies in medieval and renaissance history* **8,** 1986, 1-30.

Canterbury. Saint Augustine's Abbey
BALLARD, ADOLPHUS, ed. *An eleventh-century inquisition of St. Augustines, Canterbury.* Records of the social and economic history of England and Wales **4.II**. Oxford University Press, 1920. Bound with NEILSON, N., ed. *A Terrier of Fleet, Lincolnshire.*

TURNER, G.J., & SALTER, H.E., eds. *The register of St. Augustine's Abbey, Canterbury, commonly called the black book.* 2 vols. Records of the social and economic history of England and Wales **2-3**. Oxford University Press for the British Academy, 1915-24. Medieval estate documents *etc.*

SHERLOCK, D. 'The account of George Nycholl for St. Augustine's, 1552-1553', *A.C.* **99**, 1984, 25-46. Transcript, documenting the sale of second-hand building materials from the dissolved Abbey, with many names.

Court of record for the Liberty of the dissolved monastery of St.Augustine, 1640-1691. 396 fiche. K.F.H.S.R.P. **1483-94**. 1988. Filmed from the original manuscripts.

'The High Court of St. Augustine', *K.F.H.S.J.* **5**(10), 1989, 377-8. Lists parishes and manors owing suit to St. Augustine's, Canterbury.

Canterbury. Saint Gregory's Priory
WOODCOCK, AUDREY M., ed. *Cartulary of the Priory of St. Gregory, Canterbury.* Camden 3rd series. **88**. Royal Historical Society, 1956. Mainly relates to properties in Canterbury and East Kent.

Canterbury. Saint Laurence's Hospital
WOODRUFF, C. EVELEIGH. 'The register and chartulary of the Hospital of St. Laurence, Canterbury,' *A.C.* **50**, 1939, 33-49.

Cobham College
ARNOLD, A.A. 'Cobham College', *A.C.* **27**, 1905, 64-109. Includes list of masters, rental of college lands, 1537, and terrier of lands of the dissolved College, 1572(?)

Cumbwell Priory
'Charters of Cumbwell Priory', *A.C.* **5**, 1863, 194-222; **6**, 1866, 190-222; **8**, 1872, 271-93. Transcript of 69 charters; includes folded pedigree of Gatton, 12-13th c.

Hythe. Saint Bartholomews Hospital
RILEY, HENRY THOMAS. 'Records of the hospital of St. Bartholomew, at Hythe, Kent', HISTORICAL MANUSCRIPTS COMMISSION. *Sixth report ... Part 1: Report and appendix.* C.1745. H.M.S.O., 1877, 511-22.

Leeds Priory
SHERWOOD, LESLIE. 'The cartulary of Leeds Priory', *A.C.* **64**, 1952, 24-34. Abstracts.

Monks Horton Priory
SCOTT, JAMES R. 'Charters of Monks Horton Priory', *A.C.* **10**, 1876, 269-81. 12-14th c.

Morden College
LANSDELL, HENRY. *Princess Aelfrida's Charity.* 7 vols. Blackheath: Burnside, 1911-16. Concerns lands in Greenwich, Lewisham and Woolwich which became the endowment of Morden College; many names.

GREEN, T. FRANK. *Morden College, Blackheath.* London Survey Committee monograph **10**. 1916. Includes memorial inscriptions, biographical notes on chaplains, will of Sir John Morden, 1708, etc. The College was a home for poor merchants.

SAW, REGINALD. 'The Morden College archives', *T.G.L.A.S.* **7**(1), 1964, 25-44. Describes the extensive archival collection of this charity.

Order of Saint John of Jerusalem
COTTON, CHARLES. *A Kentish chartulary of the Order of St. John of Jerusalem.* Kent records **11** 1930. The Order held lands throughout Kent.

Ospringe. St. Mary's Hospital
DRAKE, CHARLES H. 'The Hospital of St. Mary of Ospringe, commonly called Maison Dieu', *A.C.* **38**, 1926, 113-21. Includes deed extracts, *etc.*

Rochester Archdeaconry
SIMMONS, JENNIFER G. *K.A.O. Unofficial document catalogue: Rochester Archdeaconry estates.* 2 fiche. K.F.H.S.R.P. **709**. 1986.

Rochester. Saint Bartholomew's Hospital
'Notes on hospital of St. Bartholomew, Rochester', *Kent magazine* 1, 1896, 369-88. Includes many deed abstracts; the hospital was granted to the Dean and Chapter at the dissolution.

Throwley Priory
'Notes from the chartulary of the Abbey of St. Bertin', *A.C.* 4, 1861, 203-19. 22 deeds relating to Throwley Priory, 12-13th c.

D.*Records of Particular Places*

Appledore
WINNIFRITH, JOHN, SIR. 'Land ownership in Appledore, 1500- 1900', *A.C.* 97, 1982, 1-6.

Ashford
See New Romney

Boughton Monchelsea
'Calendar of ancient deeds presented by Charles Marchant, esq.,' *A.C.* 27, 1905, 167-76. Relating to Boughton Monchelsea, 14-17th c.

Canterbury
URRY, WILLIAM. 'A 12th century rental of Christchurch, Canterbury', *Canterbury Cathedral chronicle* 40, 1944, 14-21. For Canterbury.
WOODRUFF, C. EVELEGH. 'The Parliamentary survey of the precincts of Canterbury Cathedral in the time of the Commonwealth', *A.C.* 49, 1938, 195-222.

Chilham
JESSUP, F.W., ed. 'Court rolls of the manor of Chilham, 1654-6', in *A seventeenth century miscellany.* Kent records 17, 1960, 1-34.

Cobham
'Cobham Hall', *A.C.* 11, 1877, lxv-xc. Includes extract from letters patent, 1612, naming occupiers of the estate.
HARRIS, EDWIN, *Cobham Park and estate.* Eastgate series 5. Rochester: Harris, 1905. Includes names of tenants in 1612, *etc.*

Dartford
KIRBY, J.W. *The manor house of Henry VIII at Dartford, Kent.* 4 fiche. K.F.H.S.R.P. 50. 1985. Includes transcript of accounts; many names of building tradesmen *etc.*

Deal
Abstract of the title deeds for Beach Street, Deal. 4 fiche. K.F.H.S.R.P. 1599. 1989.
Deeds from Middle Street area, Deal. 3 fiche. K.F.H.S.R.P. 1668. 1992.

Deal Prebend
S[TEBBING], W.P.D. 'A court leet and court baron record for the manor of Deal Prebend in 1708', *A.C.* 48, 1936, 253-6.

Dengemarsh
SCARGILL-BIRD, S.R., ed. *Custumals of Battle Abbey in the reign of Edward I and Edward II, 1283-1312, from mss. in the Public Record Office.* Camden Society, N.S., 41. 1887. Includes rentals and custumals of Dengemarsh and Wye in Kent. Battle Abbey is in Sussex.

East Malling
WILLIAMS, C.L. SINCLAIR. 'A rental of the manor of East Malling, A.D.1410', in HULL, F., ed. *A Kentish miscellany.* Kent records 21, 1979, 27-78.

Farnborough
BOND, B.F. 'A Farnborough (Kent) court roll of 1408', *A.C.* 57, 1945, 21-5.
BOND, M.F. 'Farnborough manor in the seventeenth and eighteenth centuries', *A.C.* 59, 1947, 7-18. Notes on the manorial court rolls, with list of records, 15-19th c.
'Farnborough (Kent), 1798', *N.W.K.F.H.* 1(3), 1979, 71. Survey of 1798, naming owners, occupiers, acreage and crops.

Grain
EVANS, JOHN H. 'The Rochester Bridge lands in Grain', *A.C.* 68, 1955, 184-96. Includes names of tenants, c.1616, 1674, 1716, and 1812.

Gravesend
HART, WILLIAM HENRY. *An enquiry into the tenure of the lands in the parish of Gravesend, Co. Kent, more especially with regard to their gavelkind and non-gavelkind qualities.* Gravesend: Thomas Hall, 1873.

Hartley

Cramp, Gerald. 'Manorial rolls: a useful genealogical source', *N.W.K.F.H.* 3(6), 1984, 202-4. Includes discussion of the roll for Hartley, 1782-1862.

Headcorn

GROVE, L.R.A. 'Kent's Charity, Headcorn, 1565', *A.C.* 65, 1953, 194-5. Brief survey, naming tenants.

Hoo

'A rentall of the mannor of Sherewscourt als Hoo in the Ile of Thanett ... 1633 ...', *Fragmenta genealogica* 7, 1902, 1-5.

Ightham

HARRISON, EDWARD. 'The court rolls and other records of the manor of Ightham as a contribution to local history', *A.C.* 48, 1936, 169-218; 49, 1938, 1-95. Extensive extracts, with lists of names.

Little Chart
See Westwell

Minster in Thanet

ALDRED, HENRY W. *The manor of Minster, and other estates, in the Isle of Thanet, in the County of Kent, compiled from original deeds and documents, examined abstracts of title, rent rolls, wills, etc.* Camberwell: the author, 1889. Includes many deed abstracts, pedigrees, *etc.*

New Romney

COCK, F. WILLIAM. 'A custumal of New Romney', *A.C.* 51, 1940, 188-90. Brief note on a 16th c. custumal.

BOOKER, JOHN M.L., ed. *The Wiston archives: a catalogue.* Chichester: West Sussex County Council, 1975. Primarily relates to Sussex, but includes listing of over 400 deeds etc., relating to New Romney, Ashford, Sittingbourne and Sevenoaks areas; also folded pedigrees of Goring, 17-20th c. and Fagge, 16-18th c.

Otford

ELLIS, HENRY, SIR. ed. 'Extent, etc., of the royal manor of Otford, 1573', *A.C.* 5, 1863, 328-30.

Plumstead

MANDY, W.H. 'The manor of Plumstead in the XIIIth and XIVth centuries', *W.D.A.S.A.R.* 17, 1912, 36-63. See also 18, 1913, 37-54, & 19, 1914, 33-49. Includes abstracts of medieval records; also list of clergy, 12-20th c., and various tax lists, 14-17th c.

VINCENT, W.T. 'The custumal of Plumstead', *W.D.A.S.A.R.* 18, 1913, 70-73. Late 13th c., includes some names of tenants.

Reculver

HUSSEY, ARTHUR. 'Ford manor house and lands in 1647', *A.C.* 26, 1904, 119-32. Survey, naming tenants at Ford and Reculver.

Ripple

NUNNS, GERTRUDE. 'Eighteenth century families involved in land transactions in Ripple & Deal', *K.F.H.S.J.* 4(9), 1985, 320-23. Extracts from deeds relating to the Larkin, Lynch, Talbot, Easly, Dispain, and Friend families, *etc.,* 18-19th c.

River Medway

'Survey of the marshes on the River Medway, *temp.* Hen. VIII or Edw. VI', *Topographer & genealogist* 2, 1853, 447-9.

Sevenoaks
See New Romney

Sittingbourne
See New Romney

Rochester. Ambree

ARNOLD, A.A. 'A fourteenth-century court roll of the manor of Ambree, Rochester', *A.C.* 29, 1911, 89-153.

Sundrish

KNOCKER, HERBERT W. 'The evolution of the Holmesdale, no.3: the manor of Sundrish', *A.C.* 44, 1932, 189-210. Includes brief list of surviving records.

Swainestrey

GRIFFIN, RALPH. 'The Lepers' Hospital at Swainestrey', *A.C.* 34, 1920, 63-78. Includes abstracts of 26 medieval deeds. At Murston.

Teynham

SELBY, ELIZABETH. *Teynham manor and hundred (798-1935).* Ashford: Headley Bros., 1936. Reprinted Rainham: Meresborough Books, 1982. Includes transcripts of the reeve's account, 1376, subsidy roll, 14th c., also notes on churchwardens' accounts, many pedigrees, list of clergy, *etc.*

Tynton

'A rentall of the mannr of Tynton ... 1612 ...', *Fragmenta genealogica* **8**, 1902, 75-6.

Westwell

L[ARKING], L.B. 'On the alienation of the manors of Westwell and Little Chart by Peter de Berding, and the tenure of the former manor', *A.C.* **6**, 1866, 305-21. Deed abstracts, 13th c.

Willesborough

FRAMPTON, T.S. 'Rent roll of the heirs of John and William de Willesborough, temp Edward II', *A.C.* **15**, 1883, 361-3. Relating to Willesborough.

Woodnesborough

S[TEBBING], W.P.D. 'Some court rolls of Woodnesborough, otherwise Winsborow', *A.C.* **51**, 1940, 219-20. Brief note, 17-19th c.

Wye

MUHLFELD, HELEN ELIZABETH. *A survey of the manor of Wye.* New York: Columbia University Press, 1933. Rental, 1452-4; extensive.
See also Dengemarsh

E. *Manorial and other descents of property*

Many works on manors and other properties trace their descent, rather than providing information on estate archives. Such works are listed here. Two general works are noted first.

OSWALD, ARTHUR. *Country houses of Kent.* Country Life, 1933. Includes brief notes on some owners.

WADMORE, J.F. 'The Knights Hospitallers in Kent', *A.C.* **22**, 1897, 232-74. Notes on the medieval descent *etc.* of the many manors owned by the Templars.

Allington Castle

CONWAY, AGNES E.'The owners of Allington Castle, Maidstone (1086-1279)', *A.C.* **29**, 1911, 1-39.

Ashford. Middle Row

BRISCALL, W.R. 'The Ashford Cage', *A.C.* **101**, 1985, 57-68. Includes descent of the property now known as 1, Middle Row.

Aylesham. Ratling Court

LOFTUS, PATRICK. 'Ratling Court, Aylesham', *K.F.H.S.J.* 1(9), 1976, 185-8. Descent.

PARKIN, E.W. 'Ratling Court, Aylesham', *A.C.* **92**, 1976, 53-64. Includes descent, 11-20th c.

Bethersden

PEARMAN, A.J. 'Notes on Bethersden', *A.C.* **27**, 1905, 201- 8. Primarily relating to property descents.

Bexley. Hall Place

MORRIS, P.E. *Hall Place, Bexley.* Bexley: Libraries and Museums Dept., 1970. Includes descent.

WOLFE, DONOVAN. 'The manor of Bexley and Hall Place', *Transaction of the Dartford District Antiquarian Society* **6**, 1936, 24-30. Descent.

Bifrons

THOMAS, B.M. 'A history of Bifrons mansion house', *A.C.* **110**, 1993, 313-29. Includes notes on descent through Bargrave, Taylor, Conyngham, *etc.*

Blackheath

RHIND, NEIL. *Blackheath village and environs 1790-1990.* Blackheath: Bookshop Blackheath, 1983-93. v.1. The village and Blackheath Vale. v.2. Wricklemarsh and the Cator Estate; Kidbrooke; Westcombe; the Angerstein encroachment (St. Johns Park). v.1. is revised ed. Extensive; traces descents of numerous properties.

Eliot Place

MARTIN, A.R. *No. 6, Eliot Place, Blackheath: the house and its occupants 1797-1972.* Greenwich and Lewisham Antiquarian Society, 1974. Includes biographical information.

Paragon House
BONWITT, W. *The history of The Paragon and Paragon House and their residents.* Blackheath: The Bookshop Blackheath, [1977?] Includes biographical notes relating to a house at Blackheath.

Park House
BAKER, L.A.J. *A house and its occupiers: Park House, Cresswell Park (St. Mary's Presbytery) Blackheath, S.E.3.* [Privately printed], [1957]. Includes biographical notes on occupiers.

Boughton Aluph
GARDINER, DOROTHY. 'The manor of Boughton Aluph and Sir Thomas de Aldon', *A.C.* **50**, 1939, 122-30. 13-14th c., includes pedigrees showing relationship of Badlesmere and Burghersh.

Brasted Place
SINGLETON, H.G.H. *Brasted Place and its owners: a short history.* [ ], [195-?]. Descent.

Bridge Place
PINHORN, MALCOLM. 'Lesser known buildings: Bridge Place, Kent', *Blackmansbury* **5**(3 & 4), 1968, 47-67. Descent, 13-20th c., includes probate inventory of Sir Arnold Braems, 1681.

Broadstairs. Pierremont Hall
OLIVER, DAVID R. 'The early history of Pierremont Hall in Broadstairs', *B.K.* **15**(3), 1994, 173-9; **15**(4), 1994, 215- 9. Descent; notes on Forsyth, Payler and Fletcher families, 18- 19th c.

Charing. Peirce House
WINZAR, PATRICIA. 'Peirce House, Charing: the house and its owners', *A.C.* **111**, 1993, 131-200. Includes pedigrees (some folded) of Rosmodres, 14-15th c., Brent, 15-16th c., Dering, 16-17th c., Sayer, 18-20th c., and Peirce, 17-19th c. Also includes various probate records.

Chislehurst
ROBERTSON, W.A. SCOTT. 'Chislehurst and its church', *A.C.* **13**, 1880, 386-403. Descent; includes pedigrees of Walsingham, 14-17th c., and of Bettenson, Selwyn and Townsend, 17-19th c.

Cobham
ARNOLD, A.A. 'Cobham and its manors *etc.* *A.C.* **27**, 1905, 110-35. Notes on the descent of the various manors in the parish; includes various rentals and surveys, giving tenants' names.
ARNOLD, RALPH. *Cobham Hall, Kent: notes on the house, its owners, the gardens and park, and objects of special interest.* Cobham: Westwood Educational Trust, [1951?] Brief notes on descent.
WALLER, J.G. 'The lords of Cobham, their monuments, and the church', *A.C.* **11** 1877, 49-112; **12**, 1878, 113-66. Descent though Cobham, De La Pole, Braybrooke, Hawberk and Brooks, medieval-17th c.

Cowden
LEVESON-GOWER, GRANVILLE. 'Notes on three ancient houses in the parish of Cowden', *A.C.* **21**, 1895, 103-8. Includes brief notes on owners, with references to many wills.

Cudham. Apuldrefield
STEINMAN, G. STEINMAN. 'Some account of the manor of Apuldrefield in the parish of Cudham, Kent', *Topographer and genealogist* **3**, 1858, 1-21 & 178-222. Includes pedigrees of Apuldrefield (medieval) and Lennard (16-17th c.)

Dane Court
HILLS, PETER J. *Dane Court, St. Peters-in-Thanet: a Kentish manor and its families.* G.W. Belton 1972. Traces descent of the manor, 14-19th c.

Dartford. Stoneham
KELLY, JOAN. 'Stanham (Stoneham) Dartford, *Dartford Historical & Antiquarian Society newsletter* **20**, 1983, 4-15. Includes descent.

Downe
ATKINS, HEDLEY, SIR. *Down: the house of the Darwins: the story of a house and the people who lived there.* Royal College of Surgeons, 1974. Traces ownership, medieval-19th c.

East Chalk. Filborough
ARNOLD, GEORGE M. 'Filborough Farmhouse, East Chalk. Gravesend', *A.C.* **21**, 1895, 161-171. Includes notes on descent, 16-17th c.

Eastwell. Lake House
PARKIN, E.W. 'The vanishing houses of Kent, 8: Lake House, Eastwell', *A.C.* **84**, 1969, 151-61. Includes manorial descent, 11-20th c.

Evegate
MACMICHAEL, N.H. 'The descent of the manor of Evegate in Smeeth, with some account of its lords', *A.C.* **74**, 1961, 1-47. Includes folded pedigrees of Grelley, 13-14th c., Pashley, 13-14th c., Sergeaux, 14th c., Pympe and Scott, 15-16th c.

Eynsford. Little Mote
HILL, R.H. ERNEST. 'Little Mote, Eynsford, with a pedigree of the Sybill family', *A.C.* **26**, 1904, 79-90. 15-16th c.

Frindsbury. Quarry House
ARNOLD, A.A. 'Quarry House, on Frindsbury Hill', *A.C.* **17**, 1887, 169-80. In Frindsbury parish. Identifies tenants, 16-19th c.

Godmersham Park
SMITHERS, DAVID WALDRON, SIR. 'Godmersham Park', *Wye local history* 2(3), 1983, 2-7. Descent; includes pedigree showing inter-relationship of Knatchbull, Brodnax and Austen.

Greenwich
KELSALL, FRANK. 'Hillside and Park Hall, Crooms Hill, Greenwich', *T.G.L.A.S.* **8**(6), 1978, 210-22. Includes descent through Dry, James, Campbell, and Sainsbury, *etc.,* 17-19th c.

Hartlip. Queensdown
See Rainham. Queens Court

Horsham
ROBERTSON, W.A. SCOTT. 'Horsham manor in Upchurch', *A.C.* **18**, 1889, 399-402. Includes names of neighbouring landowners.

Howbury
CUMBERLAND, A. 'Howbury manor', *Transactions of the Dartford District Antiquarian Society* **5**, 1935, 22-5. Descent. In Crayford parish.

Ightham Mote
WOODRUFF, C.E. 'Notes on former owners of Ightham Mote House', *A.C.* **24**, 1900, 195-200. Includes pedigree of Selby, 17-18th c.

Knole
DU BOULAY, F.R.H. 'The assembling of an estate: Knole in Sevenoaks, c.1275 to c.1525', *A.C.* **89**, 1974, 1-10. Discussion based on deeds.
Knole, Kent. National Trust, 1976. Includes notes on owners.

Lee
BIRCHENOUGH, EDWYN, & BIRCHENOUGH, JOSEPHINE. *Two old Lee houses: Dacre House and Lee House.* Borough of Lewisham, 1968. Traces descents.
BIRCHENOUGH, EDWYN, & BIRCHENOUGH, JOSEPHINE. *The Manor House, Lee.* 2nd ed. London Borough of Lewisham, 1971. Includes notes on many tenants and residents.

Leeds Castle
CLEGGETT, DAVID A.H. *History of Leeds Castle and its families.* Maidstone: Leeds Castle Foundation, 1990. Descent; includes pedigrees of Culpepper, Fairfax, Martin and Wykeham- Martin.

Lewisham. Sion House
MACARTNEY, SYLVIA. 'Sion House, Lewisham: an account of its site, some of its owners, occupants and associations', *Lewisham Local History Society transactions* 1974, 34-58.

Leybourne Castle
SAXBY, J.C.R. 'Leybourne Castle and its early owners', *Invicta magazine* **3**, 1913, 71. Brief descent to 14th c.

Lullingstone
MEATES, G.W. 'Lullingstone and its owners', *Cantium* **5**(2), 1973, 29-35. Descent.

Old Sore
WADMORE, J.F. 'The manor of Old Sore, near Plaxtol in Kent', *A.C.* **22**, 1897, 310-15. Includes notes on medieval descent, especially concerning the Colepepper family.

Otham

VAUX, HUGH. 'Otham: people and places', *A.C.* **111**, 1993, 227-36. Discussion of a project to trace the ownership and occupation of land, 1654-1851.

Oxney

HARDMAN, F.W., STEBBING, W.P.D., & GARDNER, C.H. 'The parish and reputed manor of Oxney, near Dover', *A.C.* **59**, 1947, 82-94. Includes notes on descent.

Rainham. Queen Court

FAUSSETT-OSBORNE, H.G. 'Queen Court, Rainham, and Queendown, Hartlip', *A.C.* **35**, 1921, 37-40. Notes on descent.

Reach

MACFIE, A.C. 'The manor of Reach, 1085-c.1900', *J.K.L.H.* **14**, 1982, 3-5. Descent.

Rochester
High Street

WHEATLEY, S.W. 'A house in Rochester High Street numbered 69 and 71', *A.C.* **38**, 1926, 69-74. Includes notes on descent.

Restoration House

AVELING, STEPHEN T. 'History of Restoration House, Rochester', *A.C.* **15**, 1883, 117-26. Lists owners and occupiers, 17-19th c.

Romden Place

WORSFOLD, W. BASIL. 'Romden Place and its restoration', *A.C.* **43**, 1931, 73-84. Includes notes on descent.

Roydon

COOK, A.R. *A manor through four centuries.* Oxford University Press, 1938. Study of the manor of Roydon, in Peckham; traces descent; includes pedigree of Twysden, 13-16th c.

Scotgrove

PROUDFOOT, W. FRANK. 'The manor and chantry of Scotgrove', *A.C.* **94**, 1979, 7-26. Includes notes on descent.

Shurland House

CAVE-BROWN, J. 'Shurland House', *A.C.* **23**, 1898, 86-93. Notes on descent.

Stede Hill

GOODSALL, ROBERT H. *Stede Hill: the annals of a Kentish home.* Ashford: Headley Brothers, 1949. Descent; includes folded pedigrees of Stede, 16-18th c., Horsmonden, 16-18th c., and Baldwin, 18-19th c.

Stone. Marion College

HARDING, WENDY. 'Marion College', *N.W.K.F.H.* **3**(3), 1983, 97-8. Descent of a cottage at Stone, Dartford, 18-20th c.

Sutton at Hone

MALLIK, THEADORE C. 'Owners and tenants of St. John of Jerusalem, Sutton-at-Hone, after the dissolution of the monasteries in 1540', *Dartford Historical & Antiquarian Society newsletter* **16**, 1979, 18-29. Descent.

Swingfield

WADMORE, J.F. 'Knights Hospitallers in Kent', *A.C.* **24**, 1900, 128-38. Abstracts from ministers' accounts relating to property in Swingfield, Tonbridge and West Peckham; medieval.

Tonbridge

WADMORE, J.F. 'Tonbridge Castle and its lords', *A.C.* **16**, 1886, 12-57. Medieval descent.

ELLISTON-ERWOOD, F.C. *Well Hall: the story of the house, its grounds and its famous occupants* ed. Philip C. Bursill. 3rd ed.Woolwich: Woolwich Borough Council, 1947. Descent; includes pedigree of Chichele, 1436-1731.

See also Swingfield

West Peckham. Oxenhoath

ANDREWS, H.C. 'The descent of Oxenhoath Manor, West Peckham, Kent', *A.C.* **46**, 1934, 213-4. Brief notes, 17th c., Chowne family.

LAWRENCE, MARGARET. 'The families and house of Oxenhoath, West Peckham', *A.C.* **111**, 1993, 237-62. Traces descent through Culpepper, Miller and Geary, 14-20th c.

Wombwell Hall

GREEN, E.R. 'Wombwell Hall', *Gravesend Historical Society transactions* **19**, 1973, 11-14. Descent, 16-20th c.

Woolwich
NORMAN, WM. 'The manor of Woolwich',
W.D.A.S.A.R. **5,** 1900, 31-42. Descent.

9. RECORDS OF NATIONAL AND COUNTY ADMINISTRATION

Government bureaucracy is responsible for many of the sources used by genealogists. Many publications based on these sources are listed elsewhere in this bibliography, e.g., section 7, official lists of names. Here, the intention is to identify those works which calendar records such as the Quarter Sessions rolls, which list the names of officials or which identify other people interacting with the govenmental machinery in various ways (and especially as rebels!) This section should be read in conjunction with Raymond's *English genealogy: a bibliography,* which identifies a number of more general works on the topics covered here. General works based on the public records, and which may be of genealogical use, are listed here in rough chronological order:

GREENSTREET, JAMES. 'Holders of knight's fees in Kent at the knighting of the King's son, anno 38 Henry III (A.D. 1253-4)', *A.C.* **12,** 1878, 197-237. 494 names.

GREENSTREET, JAMES. 'Fragment of the Kent portion of Kirkby's inquest temp. Edward I', *A.C.* **11,** 1877, 365-9. Lists holders of knights' fees.

MAITLAND, FREDERIC WILLIAM, HARCOURT, LEVESON WILLIAM VERNON, & BOLLAND, WILLIAM CRADDOCK, eds. *Year books of Edward II. Vol. V. The eyre of Kent, 6 & 7 Edward II, A.D. 1313-1314.* Selden Society **24, 27,** & **29.** 1910-13.

FLAHERTY, W.E. 'The Great Rebellion in Kent of 1381, illustrated from the public records', *A.C.* **3,** 1860, 65-96. See also 179-83, & **4,** 1861, 235-7. Includes 24 presentments of rebels.

FLAHERTY, W.E. 'Sequel to the Great Rebellion in Kent of 1381', *A.C.* **4,** 1861, 67-86. Summaries of trial documents.

HARVEY, I.M.W. *Jack Cade's rebellion of 1450.* Oxford: Clarendon Press, 1991. The rebellion primarily affected Kent Surrey, Sussex and Essex.

COOPER, WILLIAM DURRANT. 'John Cade's followers in Kent', *A.C.* **7,** 1868, 233-71. Primarily lists of rebels in 1450.

ORRIDGE, B.B. *Illustrations of Jack Cade's Rebellion* ... John Camden Hotten, 1869. Includes lists of Cade's followers in Kent and Sussex; also folded pedigree of Cooke of Gidea Hall, Essex, 16-19th c.

POOLE, ERIC. *Followers of John Cade's rebellion, 1450, from Kent, Sussex, Essex & Surrey.* K.F.H.S.R.P. **39**. 1985.

VIRGOE, R. 'Some ancient indictments in the King's Bench referring to Kent, 1450-1452', in DU BOULAY, F.R.H., ed. *Documents illustrative of medieval Kentish society.* Kent records **18**, 1964, 214-65.

WHYLER, FRED. 'The filth and scum of Kent', *N.W.K.F.H.* 1(5), 1980, 136. List of rebels from N.W. Kent who participated in Jack Cade's rebellion, 1450.

CONWAY, AGNES ETHEL. 'The Maidstone sector of Buckingham's Rebellion, Oct. 18, 1483', *A.C.* **37**, 1925, 97-120. Lists rebels, with biographical notes; includes pedigree of Woodville, shewing connections with the rebels.

ZELL, M.L. 'Early Tudor J.P.s at work', *A.C.* **93**, 1977, 125-43. General discussion.

CLARKE, R.D. 'West Kent Quarter-Sessions orders in the reign of Charles I', *A.C.* **80**, 1966, 227-38. General discussion.

LARKING, LAMBERT B., ed. *Proceedings, principally in the county of Kent, in connection with the parliaments called in 1640, and especially with the Committee of Religion appointed in that year.* Camden Society old series **80**. 1862. Letters, *etc.*, of Sir Edward Dering; includes petitions with many names of petitioners.

ALMACK, RICHARD. 'Papers relating to proceedings in the County of Kent, A.D.1642-A.D. 1646', in *The Camden miscellany* 3. Camden Society O.S. **61**. 1855, separately paginated. Letters and papers of the Parliamentary County Committee in the Civil War, includes account of the 'contribution and subscription money', 1642, giving names.

EVERITT, ALAN, ed. 'An account book of the Committee of Kent for 1647-1648', in *A seventeenth century miscellany.* Kent records **17**, 1960, 115-52.

COLOMB, GEORGE. 'The Royalist rising in Kent, A.D.1648', *A.C.* **9**, 1874, 31-49. Lists many names.

'North West Kent royalists', *N.W.K.F.H.* 1(3), 1979, 68. List of suspects, 1655.

WHYLER, FRED. 'Royalist sympathisers, 1655-1657', *N.W.K.F.H.* 7(3), 1995, 83-4. List for North West Kent, drawn up by the Kent County Committee.

RHODES, A. 'Suspected persons in Kent', *A.C.* **23**, 1898, 68-77. Lists suspected royalists, 1656.

KEITH-LUCAS, BRYAN. *Parish affairs: the government of Kent under George III.* [ ]: Kent County Library, 1986. Include useful list of landowners.

'Jurors of the Kent summer assizes 1835', *Topographical quarterly* 1(2), 1933, 112-6.

Members of Parliament for the shire, for New Romney, and for Rochester, are listed in three separate works:

CAVE-BROWN, J. 'Knights of the shire for Kent from A.D.1275 to A.D.1831', *A.C.* **21**, 1895, 198-243.

STOKES, JOHN. 'The barons of New Romney in Parliament, *A.C.* **27**, 1905, 44-63. Lists M.P.'s, with brief notes.

SMITH, FREDERICK FRANCIS. *Rochester in Parliament, 1295-1933, including the Chatham and Gillingham divisions of Rochester, also the Borough of Chatham from June 1832 to 1918.* Simpkin Marshall, 1933. Biographies of M.P.'s.

A list of sheriffs, 995-1795 is printed in:

PETLEY-JONES, DAVID. 'The sheriffs of Kent, 995-1795', *K.F.H.S.J.* **3-5**, 1981-9, *passim.*

For the subsequent period, see:

'Sheriffs of Kent 1796-1974', *K.F.H.S.J.* 1(2), 1975, 39-40; 1(3), 1975, 60-61.

A list of Justices of the Peace in mid-18th century Blackheath Hundred is printed in:

MONSON, LESLIE, SIR. 'Blackheath justices of the peace, 1743 to 1749', *T.G.L.A.S.* 9(4), 1982, 200-14. Includes list with biographical notes.

Assize Records

There are a number of works calendaring records of Kentish assizes. These are listed here in chronological order.

PUTNAM, BERTHA HAVEN, ed. *Kent keepers of the peace, 1316-1317.* Kent records **13.** 1933. Primarily an edition of the assize rolls.

COCKBURN, J.S., ed. *Calendar of assize records: Kent indictments, Elizabeth I.* H.M.S.O., 1979.

COCKBURN, J.S., ed. *Calendar of assize records: Kent indictments, James I.* H.M.S.O., 1980.

COCKBURN, J.S., ed. *Calendar of assize records: Kent indictments, Charles I.* H.M.S.O., 1995.

COCKBURN, J.S., ed. *Calendar of assize records: Kent indictments, 1649-1659.* H.M.S.O., 1989.

KNAFLA, LOUIS A. *Kent at law 1602: the county jurisdiction: assizes and sessions of the peace.* H.M.S.O., 1995. Extensive calendar of court records.

MANDY, W.H. 'A Kentish hundred: pleas of the Crown for the Hundred of Ruxley with a running commentary', *Journal of the British Archaeological Association* N.S., **22,** 1916, 245-54. Assize roll, 1227.

Quarter Sessions

The records of Quarter and Petty Sessions are extensive, and are calendared in a number of works:

Calendar of Quarter Sessions records, 1574-1622. 4 vols. [Maidstone]: Kent County Council, 1976.

Calendar of early Quarter Sessions rolls, 1596-1605. [Maidstone]: Kent County Council, [1975?]

K.A.O. *Quarter sessions catalogues ...* Fiche. K.F.H.S.R.P. **650-58.** 1986.

Calendar of Quarter Sessions records 1574-1622. 13 fiche. K.F.H.S.R.P. **468-9.** 1987.

Calendar of early Quarter Sessions rolls 1596-1605. 4 fiche. K.F.H.S.R.P. **466.** 1986.

Calendar of Quarter Sessions records: sessions papers, 1639-1677. 3 fiche. K.F.H.S.R.P. **467.** 1986.

Calendar of Quarter Sessions records. 10 fiche. K.F.H.S.R.P. **1653-5.** 1992. For 1639-1715.

Calendar of Quarter Sessions records. Sessions papers 1639-1677. Kent County Council, 1978.

HARRINGTON, DUNCAN W. *Geneal [sic] sessions of the peace and gaol delivery held at the Guildhall, Canterbury, 1751-1759, for the City of Canterbury and County of the same city.* 3 fiche. K.F.H.S.R.P. **164.** 1985.

Catalogue: petty sessions records, lieutenancy & shrivalty. 3 fiche. K.F.H.S.R.P. **702.** 1986.

SHORROCKS, DEREK M.M. 'Eighteenth century petty sessions: records in Kent', *Society of Local Archivists bulletin* **14,** 1954, 10-12.

Lieutenancy Records

THOMSON, GLADYS SCOTT, ed. *The Twysden Lieutenancy papers 1583-1668.* Kent records **10.** 1926.

Charity Commissioners

CHARITY COMMISSIONERS. *The charities in the county of Kent.* James Newman, 1839. Reports of 1815-39.

Commissioners for Sewers

K.A.O. *catalogues. Records of Commissioners for Sewers.* 4 fiche. K.F.H.S.R.P. **748.** 1986.

LONDON COUNTY COUNCIL. *Court minutes of the Surrey & Kent Sewer Commission, Volume 1, comprising the minutes of the first two commissions whose records exist, and covering the period from 1569 to 1579 ...* London County Council, 1909.

K.A.O. *Medway area rivers and sewers records ...* 4 fiche. K.F.H.S.R.P. **747.** 1986. Includes rentals, wages books, minutes, etc., mainly 20th c.

Coroners' Records

K.A.O. *catalogues: coroners records ...* 3 fiche. K.F.H.S.R.P. **764.** 1986. Also lists valuation records of the Land Value Duty, early 20th c., and various other collections.

Turnpike Records

Turnpike records T/1-22, highway boards. 2 fiche. K.F.H.S.R.P. **772.** 1986. Includes accounts, letters, minute books, *etc.*

WHYLER, FRED. 'Roads' *N.W.K.F.H.* **5**(8), 1990, 283-7. Includes list of trustees of the Farnborough to Riverhill road, 1747.

Charity Records

Charity records Ch.1-Ch.[46] (K.A.O. catalogues). 6 fiche. K.F.H.S.R.P. **739-41.** 1986. Lists deeds, accounts, rentals etc., of various charities.

Poor Law Records

Poor law records for Kent are extensive and important for genealogists. A general survey is provided by Melling's *Kentish sources IV* (see above, p. 10). Published records for particular places are listed in section 11 below. For a listing of the holdings available at the Centre for Kentish Studies, see: *K.A.O. Guardian and poor law union records ...* 5 fiche. K.F.H.S.R.P. **745-6.** 1986.

A detailed and important guide to Kent settlement records is provided by:

RICKARD, GILLIAN. *Kent settlement (poor law) records: a guide and catalogue.* 2 vols. Canterbury: the author, 1993-4. Pt.1. East Kent (Diocese of Canterbury). Pt.2. West Kent (Diocese of Rochester.) A supplement to part 1 was published 1997.

Reference may also be made to two other works on settlement certificates:

FIELD, E.H. *East Kent settlement certificates, part 1: parishes of Chislet, Petham, Reculver and Sturry.* 2 fiche. K.F.H.S.R.P. **42.** 1985.

'East Kent settlement and removal index', *Ancestor: quarterly journal of the Genealogical Society of Victoria* **21**(5), 1993, 9-10. Description of Gillian Rickard's index to settlement examinations, bonds, removal orders, *etc.,* 17-19th c.

Other works on the Poor Law include:

COLE, JEAN. 'Yet another source for finding a missing ancestor',*N.W.K.F.H.* **6**(8), 1993/4, 262-3. Extracts from *The poor law unions gazette* for 1858, listing advertisements for Kentish absconders.

COLE, JEAN A. 'Kent vagrants in Wiltshire', *N.W.K.F.H.* **5**(4) 2989, 141-3. Extracts from various lists of the poor in Salisbury, early 17th c.

COOKE, RICHARD. 'The Palatines', *A.C.* **26,** 1904, 321-5. Certificates from the churchwardens of various Kent parishes, refusing to accept Palatine refugees, i.e. German protestants, 1709. Give names of churchwardens and some parishioners.

Cinque Ports

BROOKS, FREDERICK W. 'The Cinque Ports', *Mariners mirror* **15**, 1929, 142-91. General study.

HULL, FELIX, ed. *A calendar of the white and black books of the Cinque Ports, 1432-1955.* Kent records **19**. 1966. Also published as HISTORICAL MANUSCRIPTS COMMISSION. *Joint publication* **5**. H.M.S.O., 1966.

Catalogue of archives of the Confederation and of the Lord Warden of the Cinque Ports. 3 fiche. K.F.H.S.R.P. **465.** 1986.

PHILIPOT, JOHN. *John Philipot's Roll of the Constables of Dover Castle and Land Wardens of the Cinque Ports 1627,* ed. Francis W. Steer. G.Bell and Sons, 1956. See also under individual ports in section 11.

10. PAROCHIAL AND BOROUGH ADMINISTRATION

The records of parochial and borough administration — the accounts of overseers, churchwardens, and other officers, the minutes of vestries, rate lists, deeds, *etc., etc.,* contain much information of genealogical value. Records held in the Centre for Kentish Studies are listed in:
K.A.O. Borough Council records catalogues. K.F.H.S.R.P. 720-32. 1986. Contents:
720. Dartford to Deal. 3 fiche.
721-3. Faversham. 10 fiche.
724. Gravesend to New Romney. 3 fiche.
725-7. New Romney. 9 fiche.
728. Queenborough. 3 fiche.
729. Rochester to Romney Marsh. 3 fiche.
730-31. Sandwich. 5 fiche.
732. Tenterden to Tunbridge Wells. 2 fiche.
K.A.O. parish cat ... Fiche. K.F.H.S.R.P. 659-76. 1986. Lists records from Kent parish chests.
For records at Canterbury, see:
C.A.L.C. parish record catalogue. 21 fiche. K.F.H.S.R.P. 950-59. [1986?]
Records from the Urban and Rural District Councils of the late 19th and early 20th centuries may also prove useful. These are listed in:
Rural District catalogues. 8 fiche. K.F.H.S.R.P. 716-7. 1986. 19-20th c. records.
Urban District Council catalogues. 6 fiche. K.F.H.S.R.P. 718-9. 1986.

Acol

Acol, St. Mildred overseers account 1623-1720. 6 fiche. K.F.H.S.R.P. 503. 1986. Filmed from the original accounts. Continued as follows:
504. 1722-1778. 4 fiche.
505. 1777-1821. 6 fiche.
506. 1821-1834. 5 fiche.
507. 1826-1910. 9 fiche.
See also Birchington

Ash

NEWMAN, ANTHEA E. 'Removal and settlement in the parish of Ash, 1670-1834', *Cantium* 2(3), 1970, 60-71. General study.

Ashford

St. Mary, Ashford, church property deeds, 1567-1787. 5 fiche. K.F.H.S.R.P. 1595. [199-]. Filmed from the original deeds.
St. Mary, Ashford, churchwardens' accounts, 1589-1592. 3 fiche. K.F.H.S.R.P. 1582. [199-]. Filmed from the original accounts.
St. Mary, Ashford, churchwardens' accounts' &c., 1682-1779. 41 fiche. K.F.H.S.R.P. 1583. 1989. Filmed from the original accounts.
St. Mary, Ashford relief & workhouse papers, 1743-1888. 6 fiche. K.F.H.S.R.P. 1596. 1989. Filmed from the original papers.
St. Mary, Ashford, vestry minutes 1757-[1882]. 110 fiche. K.F.H.S.R.P. 1584, 1587-9 & 1592-4. [199-] filmed from the original minutes.
St. Mary, Ashford poor rate book 1803-1816. 46 fiche. K.F.H.S.R.P. 1585. [199-] Filmed from the original manuscript.
St. Mary, Ashford churchwardens' rates &c., 1821-1829. 21 fiche. K.F.H.S.R.P. 1586. [199-] Filmed from the original manuscript.
St. Mary, Ashford vestry minutes 1826-1859. 20 fiche. K.F.H.S.R.P. 1587. [199-]. Filmed from the original minutes. Continued by :
1588. 1824-1853. 15 fiche.
1589. 1832-1835. 24 fiche.
1592. 1853-1880. 16 fiche.
1593. 1860-1914. 13 fiche.
1594. 1880-1882. 2 fiche.
St. Mary, Ashford overseers' letter bk. 1830-3. 9 fiche. K.F.H.S.R.P. 1591. [199-]. Filmed from the original letter book.
St. Mary, Ashford churchwardens' rates &c., 1841-1889. 35 fiche. K.F.H.S.R.P., 1590. [199-] Filmed from the original manuscript.

Birchington

All Saints, Birchington vestry book, 1735-1838. 4 fiche. K.F.H.S.R.P. 538. 1986. Filmed from the original manuscript.
Birchington churchwardens accounts, 1531-[1765]. 16 fiche. K.F.H.S.R.P. 852-4. 1986.
Birchington and Wood/Acol churchwardens' accounts 1745 to 1825. 7 fiche. K.F.H.S.R.P. 855. 1986.

Birchington surveyors accounts 1805-1845. 4
fiche. K.F.H.S.R.P. **509**. 1986. Filmed from
the original accounts.
Birchington overseers accounts, 1620-76. 7
fiche. K.F.H.S.R.P. **497**. 1986. Filmed from
the original accounts. Continued by:
   498. 1738-1769. 6 fiche.
   499. 1769-1788. 5 fiche.
   500. 1788-1818. 9 fiche.
   501. 1808-1820. 5 fiche.
   502. 1818-1832. 8 fiche.
Birchington Workhouse accounts, 1794-1835.
3 fiche. K.F.H.S.R.P. **508**. 1986. Filmed
from the orginal acounts.
*All Saints, Birchington Workhouse acounts
1820-1835.* 6 fiche. K.F.H.S.R.P. **537**. 1986.
Filmed from the original manuscript.
*Birchington apprenticeship indentures, 1633-
1838.* 3 fiche. K.F.H.S.R.P. **856**. 1986.
All Saints, Birchington, poor rate 1835-8. 2
fiche. K.F.H.S.R.P. **536**. 1986. Filmed from
the original manuscript.
*All Saints, Birchington, church accounts
1836-1931.* 3 fiche. K.F.H.S.R.P. **535**. 1986.
Filmed from the original accounts.
*All Saints, Birchington, overseers accounts
1611-1617.* 2 fiche. K.F.H.S.R.P. **539**. 1986.
Filmed from typescript.
*All Saints, Birchington, docs. relating to the
Workhouse & Poor Law, 18th & 19th cent.*
3 fiche. K.F.H.S.R.P. **541**. 1986. Filmed
from the original manuscripts.

Bromley

'Bromley settlement certificates', *N.W.K.F.H.*
1(3), 1979, 61-4. Lists 142 certificates.
WHYLER, FRED. 'Bromley churchwardens and
overseers. 1738 to 1805', *N.W.K.F.H.* 5(3),
1989, 102-3. List.
WHYLER, FRED. 'Bromley surveyors of the
highways 1737-1805', *N.W.K.F.H.* 5(6),
1990, 217-8. List.
SILVERTHORNE, ELIZABETH. *Bromley
settlement examinations 1747-1787 & 1816-
1831.* Croydon: North West Kent F.H.S.,
1985.
*Bromley settlement examinations 1747-1787
& 1816-1831: index.* [ ]: N.W.K.F.H.S., [199-?]
HOLWORTHY, F.M.R. 'Bromley College register,
1679-1800', *Pedigree register* **2**, 1910-13,
284-6, 300-3, 333-7 and 352. Home for
clergymen's widows;, transcript of register
of admissions and deaths.

WHYLER, FRED. 'Bromley's declaration of
loyalty, 1792', *N.W.K.F.H.* 2(1), 1981, 10-15.
Lists 326 inhabitants who declared their
loyalty.

Canterbury

A number of lists and discussions of the
city's archives are available:
SHEPPARD, J. BRIGSTOCKE. 'The records of
the City of Canterbury', in HISTORICAL
MANUSCRIPTS COMMISSION. *Ninth report
... Part 1. Report and appendix.* H.M.S.O.,
1883, 129-77.
WRIGHT, THOMAS. 'On the municipal archives
of the City of Canterbury', *Archaeologia*
31, 1846, 298-211.
C.A.L.C. catalogue: City records. 3 fiche.
K.F.H.S.R.P. **964**. [1986?] Of Canterbury.
SHEPPARD, J.B. 'Report of an examination of
the historical mss. belonging to the Dean
and Chapter of Canterbury', in
HISTORICAL MANUSCRIPTS COMMISSION.
*Fifth report ... Part 1. Report and
appendix.* C1432. H.M.S.O., 1876,
427-62.
PLOMER, HENRY R. *Short account of the
records of Canterbury.* Canterbury: Cross
and Jackson, 1892
Various lists of freemen and city oficers,
etc., have been published:
URRY, WILLIAM, & BUNCE, CYPRIAN
RONDEAU. et al. *The chief citizens
of Canterbury: a list of portreeves
(prefects, prepositi) from A.D.780
until c.1100, of prepositi (bailiffs) from
the 12th century until 1448, and of
mayors from 1448 until 1978.*
[Canterbury]: Canterbury City Council,
[1978].
PETLEY-JONES, DAVID. 'Sheriffs of
Canterbury', 1461-1831', *K.F.H.S.J.* 5(12),
1989, 448-50. List.
BUTCHER, A.F. 'Canterbury's earliest rolls of
freemen admissions 1297-1363: a
reconsideration', in HULL, F., ed. *A
Kentish miscellany.* Kent records **21**. 1979,
1-26. Notes many corrections to the text
printed in:
THRUPP, SYLVIA L. 'The earliest Canterbury
freemen's rolls, 1298-1363', in DU BOULAY,
F.R.H., ed. *Documents illustrative of
medieval Kentish society.* Kent records **18**,
1964, 173-213.

COWPER, JOSEPH MEADOWS. *The roll of the freemen of the City of Canterbury, from A.D.1392 to 1800.* Canterbury: Cross and Jackman, 1903.

COWPER, J.M. *Intrantes: a list of persons admitted to live and trade within the City of Canterbury, on payment of an annual fine, from 1392 to 1592.* Canterbury: Cross & Jackman, 1904.

CORPE, STELLA, & OAKLEY, M., *The freemen of Canterbury, 1800-1835 compiled from Canterbury City Archives.* Canterbury: Kent Record Collections, 1990.

A number of individual documents have been edited:

PANTON, F.H. 'The finances and government of the City and County of Canterbury in the eighteenth and early nineteenth centuries', *A.C.* **109**, 1992, 191-246. Includes chamberlains' accounts, 1740/41 and 1745/6, listing tenants; estate survey of 1797; court leet of Westgate Ward, 1757; *etc.*

PANTON, F.H. 'Finances and government of Canterbury, early to mid-nineteenth century', *A.C.* **112**, 1994, 25-54. Includes survey of estates 1828/9, with notes on mid-19th c. purchasers; list of aldermen and councillors, 1835, *etc.*

COUSINS, DAVID. 'The Canterbury Workhouse: inmates 1832', *K.F.H.S.J.* **7**(9), 1994, 309-11. List of 213 inmates and 16 blue coat boys.

Holy Cross

COWPER, JOSEPH M. *Our parish books and what they tell us: Holy Cross, Westgate, Canterbury.* 2 vols. Canterbury: Cross & Jackman, 1885. Many extracts from parish registers, overseers accounts, churchwardens accounts, *etc.*

St. Andrew

COTTON, CHARLES. 'Churchwardens' accounts of the parish of St. Andrew, Canterbury, from A.D.1485 to A.D.1625', *A.C.* **32**, 1917, 181-246; **33**, 1918, 1-62; **34**, 1920, 1-46; **35**, 1921, 41-108; **36**, 1923, 81-122. Reprinted Mitchell, Hughes and Clarke, 1916.

St. Dunstan

COWPER, JOSEPH MEADOWS. *Accounts of the churchwardens of St. Dunstan's, Canterbury, A.D.1484-1580.* Mitchell and Hughes, 1885. Also printed in *A.C.* **16**, 1886, 289-321; **17**, 1887, 77-152.

St. Margaret Street

BURNS, MARGARET. 'Residents of St. Margarets Street, Canterbury', *K.F.H.S.J.* **5**(9), 1988, 334-7. List, 18-19th c.

Chatham

FOSTER, RONALD. *Chatham 100: a complete directory of councillors, alderman and mayors of the Borough of Chatham 1890-1974, to which is added a list of freemen of the borough and lords of the manor.* Rochester: Rochester upon Medway City Council, 1974.

Chiddingstone

GIBBONS, JUNE. 'Chiddingstone early poor law accounts', *A.C.* **73**, 1960, 193-5. Brief discussion.

Chilham

Chilham photocopies: deeds, maps, parish magazines, etc. 4 fiche. K.F.H.S.R.P. **1665**. 1992. Filmed from the original documents.

Coldred

Coldred, Kent, overseers' accounts 1718-1741, including burials 1718-1740. 3 fiche. K.F.H.S.R.P. **315**. 1986. For accounts, 1760-1806, and burials, 1760-97, see **316** (5 fiche); for accounts 1807-36, **317** (3 fiche). Filmed from the original manuscripts.

Coldred, Kent, vestry minutes 1854-92; bills & receipts 1909-10. 2 fiche. K.F.H.S.R.P. **314**. 1986. Filmed from the original manuscripts.

Cowden

EWING, GUY. *A history of Cowden.* Tunbridge Wells: Courier Co., [1926]. Includes chapters on the 'rectors and registers', 'churchwardens' accounts', and 'further parish accounts and books'.

SMALLFIELD, J.S. 'Assessment of the parish of Cowden, A.D. 1599', *A.C.* **11**, 1877, 392-3.

Crockenhill

See Farningham

Dartford

PORTEUS, G.H. 'Dartford Workhouse, 1729-1836', *Dartford Historical & Antiquarian Society news-letter* **9**, 1972, 15-33. General discussion.

Deal

DEAL AND WALMER LOCAL HISTORY RESEARCH GROUP. *The parochial records of St. Leonards, Deal, Kent.* K.F.H.S.R.P. **168**, 1985. Calendar of various records, e.g. settlement papers, apprenticeship bonds, churchwardens accounts, *etc.*

Churchwardens accounts of St. Leonards, Deal, Kent, 1636-1702; also includes later memorials and a listing of brief [sic] collected between 1665 & 1670, a list of those giving money 25 Dec 1670, signatures parishioners 8 May 1696. 2 fiche. K.F.H.S.R.P. **170**. 1985. From the original manuscripts.

St. Leonard, Deal, parochial records ... 13 fiche. K.F.H.S.R.P. **181**. 1985. Includes various tax assessments, vestry minutes, pre-marital affidavits, *etc.*

St. Leonard, Deal: churchwardens accounts and assessments, 1719-1759. 11 fiche. K.F.H.S.R.P. **399**. 1986. For 1760-1770, see **400** (8 fiche); 1696-1794, **401** (17 fiche). Filmed from the original manuscripts.

St. Leonard, Deal, churchwardens & overseers accounts & assessments 1704-1773. 11 fiche. K.F.H.S.R.P. **264**. 1986. Filmed from the original manuscripts.

St. Leonard, Deal, churchwardens & overseers accounts & assessments, 1773-1783. 10 fiche. K.F.H.S.R.P. **274**. 1986. Filmed from the original manuscripts.

St. Leonard, Deal, churchwardens & overseers accounts & assessments, 1783-89. 13 fiche. K.F.H.S.R.P. **406**. 1986. For 1802-28, see **407** (15 fiche). Filmed from the original manuscripts.

St. Leonard, Deal, Kent. Poor law assessment registers (1). 6 April 1725 to 10 March 1725/6. (2). 22 April 1729. 3 fiche. K.F.H.S.R.P. **207**. 1985. Filmed from the original manuscripts.

DALTON, JOSEPHINE, & NUNNS, GERTRUDE. eds. *An assessment made in the Vestry Room in the parish church of Deal for the relief of the poor ... April 9th 1801.* 1 fiche. K.F.H.S.R.P. **1681**. 1992. Incorrectly described on the head of the fiche as the '1801 census of Deal'.

St. Leonard, Deal: bonds for bastardy, settlement, maintenance, removal, & miscellaneous, with a calendar. 4 fiche.

K.F.H.S.R.P. **403**. 1986. Filmed from the original manuscripts.

Vestry minutes and accounts. Volume 1. Sacrament collections, 1719 to 1758; officers chosen for the parish 1721 to 1778. Reverse: disbursements of the overseers of the poor, 1694 to 1701. List of briefs and sums collected 1719 to 1774. Volume 2. Vestry minutes 1831 to 1934. Reverse: copies of the 1801, 1811, 1821 and 1831 census returns. 8 fiche. K.F.H.S.R.P. **172**. 1985. For St. Leonard, Deal. From the original manuscripts.

Vestry minutes of St. Leonard, Deal, Kent. Volume 1: 1700-1758; at rear of volume in reverse, a register of settlement certificates 1669-1771. Volume 2: 1759-1808; the minutes contain the churchwardens accounts from 1766 onwards. 6 fiche. K.F.H.S.R.P. **171**. 1985. From the original manuscripts.

DEAL AND WALMER LOCAL HISTORY RESEARCH GROUP. *Index and correlation of the 1821 census & poor law assessment for St. Leonard, Deal, Kent.* 2 fiche. K.F.H.S.R.P. **240**. 1986.

Dover

JONES, JOHN BAVINGTON. *The records of Dover: the charters, records books and papers of the Corporation, with the Dover customal.* Dover: Dover Express, 1920.

KNOCKER, EDWARD. *A lecture on the archives of the Cinque port and borough of Dover ...* Dover: Standard Office, 1878.

KNOCKER, EDWARD. 'The archives of the borough of Dover', *Journal of the British Archaeological Association* **40**, 1884, 1-14.

SCALLY, M. *Catalogue of records of Dover Harbour Board.* 2 fiche. K.F.H.S.R.P. **464**. 1986. Includes estate records, *etc.*

SIMS, R. 'Dover records in the British Museum', *Journal of the British Archaeological Association* **40**, 1884, 129-32.

STATHAM, S.P.H. 'Dover chamberlain's accounts, 1365-67', *A.C.* **25**, 1902, 75-87.

STATHAM, SAMUEL PERCY HAMMOND, ed. *Dover charters and other documents in the possession of the Corporation of Dover.* J.M. Dent & Co., 1902.

STEBBING, W.P.D. 'Bribery in an election for Dover in 1728', *A.C.* **64,** 1952, 176-7. Lists of bribes given to freemen.
Minute book, Dover Court of Lodemanage, 25 Mar. 1673 to 22 Oct. 1808. 5 fiche. K.F.H.S.R.P. **849.** 1986.

Eastry
Eastry, Kent, settlement certificates. 3 fiche. K.F.H.S.R.P. **1062.** 1987. Filmed from the original certificates.

East Greenwich
KIRBY, J.W. 'The churchwardens' accounts of the parish of St. Alfege, East Greenwich, 1630-1640', *T.G.L.A.S.* **4**(6), 1952-3, 270-84. Brief abstracts.
Numerous properties at home and overseas were held 'as of the manor of East Greenwich'. There are three articles which explain this legal fiction:
CARR, C.T. 'Our manor of East Greenwich', *Law quarterly review* **29,** 1913, 349-53.
CHEYNEY, E.P. 'The manor of East Greenwich in the County of Kent', *American historical review* **11,** 1905/6, 29-35.
HURSTFIELD, JOEL. 'The Greenwich tenures of the reign of Edward VI', *Law quarterly review* **65,** 1949, 72-81.

Edenbridge
LEVESON-GOWER, GRANVILLE. 'Churchwardens' accounts, Edenbridge', *A.C.* **21,** 1895, 118-25. Brief extracts, 17-19th c.

Elham
The churchwardens' accounts of Elham, Kent, 1729-1754; briefs 1729-48 & memoranda. 8 fiche. K.F.H.S.R.P. **296.** 1986. Filmed from the original manuscripts.
The churchwardens' accounts of Elham, Kent, 1754-1787, & vestry minutes 1759-66. 7 fiche. K.F.H.S.R.P. **295.** 1986. Filmed from the original manuscripts. For accounts, 1787-1832, see **297** (6 fiche); 1833-89, **298** (5 fiche)

The overseers accounts of Elham, Kent, 1729-1737. 6 fiche. K.F.H.S.R.P. **299.** 1986.
Continued by:
　300. 1740-51 (including vestry minutes 1743-8). 10 fiche.
　301. 1751-61 (including vestry minutes, 1751-61. 11 fiche.
　302. 1774-77. 10 fiche.
　303. 1783-91. 9 fiche.
　304. 1799-1804. 5 fiche.
　305. 1804-21. 9 fiche.
Elham vestry minute book for the years 1773-1787. 7 fiche. K.F.H.S.R.P. **307.** 1986. Filmed from the original manuscripts.
Continued by:
　308. 1788-1803. 5 fiche.
　306. 1821-34. 7 fiche.

Eltham
CORNER, G.R. 'Extracts from the churchwardens' accounts of the parish of Eltham in Kent', *Archaeologia* **34,** 1852, 51-65.
VALLANCE, AYMER. 'Eltham churchwardens' accounts', *A.C.* **47,** 1935, 71-102; **48,** 1936, 120-50. 1554-69.

Eynsford
See Farningham

Farningham
HARDING, HILARY, & HARDING, WILFRID. *The charities of Farningham and Eynsford, with Crockenhill and Lullingstone.* Publications **9.** [Farningham]: Farningham & Eynsford Local History Society, 1994. Detailed accounts of many charities; notes many names.

Faversham
RILEY, HENRY THOMAS. 'The Corporation of Faversham', in HISTORICAL MANUSCRIPTS COMMISSION. *Sixth report ... Part I: Report and appendix.* C1745. H.M.S.O., 1877, 500-11.
DANE, HERBERT. *The mayoralty of Faversham.* Faversham papers **1.** 2nd ed. Faversham: Faversham Society, 1965. Includes biographical notes on selected mayors, but not a complete list.
GIRAUD, F.F. 'Faversham town accounts, anno. 33 Edw I', *A.C.* **10,** 1886, 221-32.
GIRAUD, FRANCIS F. 'Municipal archives of Faversham A.D.1304-24', *A.C.* **14,** 1882, 185-205. Transcripts of various accounts and tax lists.

GIRAUD, F.F. 'Cinque ports: notes from minute books of the Corporation of Faversham', *A.C.* **28**, 1909, 28-74. Extracts, 16-18th c.

TELFER, W. 'Faversham's Court of Orphans', *A.C.* **81**, 1967, 191-202. Discussion based on a 16th c. manuscript.

GIRAUD, F.F. 'Extracts from the Faversham archives', *A.C.* **24**, 1900, 181-8. Includes roll of 'soldyers which serve in the general bande', 1595.

GIRAUD, F.F. 'Cinque Ports, Faversham: copy of a parchment roll with corporation seal attached, containing orders of Faversham wardmote for a cesse for shipping in 38th year of reign of Queen Elizabeth, and names of persons charged', *A.C.* **32**, 1917, 303-16.

GIRAUD, F.F. 'Expenses of the Corporation of Faversham, temp Hen.VIII', *A.C.* **10**, 1876, 233-41.

GIRAUD, F.F. 'Payments by the town of Faversham in 1635-6, extracted from the Chamberlain's accounts, and notes theron chiefly from the Wardmote Book', *A.C.* **24**, 1900, 237-43.

SMYTH, SHIRLEY. *The Faversham poor in the 18th and early 19th centuries.* Faversham papers **28**. Faversham: Faversham Society 1987. General study.

Faversham borough records: Addn. Cat. 1 fiche. K.F.H.S.R.P. **1695**. 1993. Not seen.

Folkestone

BLOOMFIELD, PETER E. *Records of Folkestone Corporation.* 14 fiche. K.F.H.S.R.P. **752-5**. 1986.

BUCHANAN, A.C.B. *The parish church, Folkestone: accounts of churchwardens 1487-1590: a link with the Tudors.* Folkestone: F.J. Parsons. [18--?] Brief extracts only.

LAXON, COLIN. 'The accounts of Folkestone parish church, 1498-1590', *B.K.* **14**(11), 1993, 647-51. General discussion.

Fordwich

SHEPPARD, J.B. 'The historical manuscripts belonging to the corporation of Fordwich in Kent', in HISTORICAL MANUSCRIPTS COMMISSION. *Fifth report ... Part 1. Report and appendix.* C1432. H.M.S.O., 1876, 606-8.

WOODRUFF, C. EVELEIGH. 'Fordwich municipal records', *A.C.* **18**, 1889, 78-102.

WOODRUFF, C. EVELEIGH. *A history of the town and port of Fordwich, with a transcription of the XVth century copy of the custumal.* Canterbury: Cross & Jackman, 1895. Includes list of mayors, muster rolls of 1573 and 1614, many wills, list of rectors, monumental inscriptions, extracts from parish registers *etc., etc.*

Catalogue of the Fordwich borough records. 6 fiche K.F.H.S.R.P. **893**. [198-?]

Fordwich borough records. 72 fiche. K.F.H.S.R.P. **967-77**. [198-?]

Fordwich parish records: churchwardens' accounts, 1814-1926. 8 fiche. K.F.H.S.R.P. **901**. [198-]. Filmed from the original accounts.

Fordwich parish records: churchwardens' inventory, faculties, correspondence and miscellaneous documents. 2 fiche. K.F.H.S.R.P. **902**. [198-]. Filmed from the original manuscripts. Numbered **903** in error.

Fordwich parish records: vestry minutes 1931-55; overseers' acounts 1790-1837. 13 fiche. K.F.H.S.R.P. **903**. [198-]. Filmed from the original manuscripts.

Gravesend

SHRIMP, A. 'Some extracts from the Gravesend Corporation records', *Invicta magazine* **1**, 1908, 40-42 & 92-3. Late 16th-17th c.

Greenwich

FRY, CYRIL. 'An old Greenwich Workhouse minute', *T.G.L.A.S.* **8**(3), 1975, 103-6. Brief notes on a minute book of 1797-8.

KIMBELL, JOHN. *An account of the legacies, gifts, rents, fees &c., appertaining to the church and poor of the parish of St. Alphege, Greenwich, in the County of Kent ...* Greenwich: [ ], 1816.

MANDY, W.H. 'Notes from the Kent Assize rolls relating to Greenwich and neighbourhood', *A.C.* **1**(3), 1912, 133-54; **1**(4), 1913, 202-22 ; **1**(5), 1914, 282-312 ; **1**(6), 1915, 373-96. Mainly 13-14th c., but includes 14-17th c., subsidies etc.

MATTHEWS, M.C. 'The charitable institutions of Greenwich parish one hundred years ago', *T.G.L.A.S.* **3**(6), 1935, 276-93.

Hawkhurst

LIGHTFOOT, W.J. 'Notes from the records of Hawkhurst church', *A.C.* **5**, 1863, 55-86. Extracts from churchwardens' accounts, 1515-1714, *etc.*

Hythe

RILEY, HENRY THOMAS. 'The manuscripts of the Corporation of Hythe, Kent', in HISTORICAL MANUSCRIPTS COMMISSION. *Fourth report ... Part 1: Report and appendix.* C857. H.M.S.O., 1874, 429-39. 'Hythe churchwardens' accounts in the time of Henry IV', *A.C.* **10**, 1876, 242-9.

Ightham

CONSTANT, JOHN. Ightham: an account book 1750-54', *A.C.* **7**, 1962, 212-4. Description of the account book of the rector, William Halford.

HARRISON, EDWARD, SIR. 'Some records of Ightham parish', *A.C.* **53**, 1941, 17-43. Brief note including extracts from accounts, early 18th c.

Lee

WOOD, A.W. 'The archives of St. Margaret's church, Lee', *Lewisham Local History Society transactions* 1968, 1-8. Discussion of records in the parish chest.

WOOD, ALFRED W. 'Lee charities and their benefactors', *Lewisham Local History Society transactions* 1981, 1-15.

Lewisham

BIRCHENOUGH, JOSEPHINE. 'Poor, but mobile', *N.W.K.F.H.* **4**(6), 1987, 209-12. Brief discussion of records relating to Lewisham.

Lullingstone

See Farningham

Lydd

FINN, ARTHUR, ed. *Records of Lydd.* Ashford: Kentish Express, 1911. Mainly the chamberlain's account book, 15th c., and the churchwardens acounts, 16th c.

RILEY, HENRY THOMAS. 'The Corporation of Lydd, Kent', in HISTORICAL MANUSCRIPTS COMMISSION. *Fifth report ... Part 1. Report and appendix.* C1432. H.M.S.O., 1876, 516-33.

STRINGER, HENRY. 'Lydd records', *A.C.* **13**, 1880, 250-55. Brief note on archives.

All Saints, Lydd, church rate book, vestry minutes & settlement certs., 1733-1792. 8 fiche. K.F.H.S.R.P. **457**. 1986. See also **458** (10 fiche) for the church rate book and churchwardens' accounts 1792-1830, and **459** (6 fiche) for 1863-80. Filmed from the original manuscripts.

All Saints, Lydd, vestry minutes, 1821-26. 5 fiche. K.F.H.S.R.P. **510**. 1986. Continued for 1874-1921 in **511**. (3 fiche). Filmed from the original minutes.

All Saints, Lydd, P.C.C. K.F.H.S.R.P. **512** & **522**. 1986. Contents: **512**. 1920-49 (7 fiche); **522**. 1962-72. (7 fiche). Filmed from the original minutes.

All Saints, Lydd, churchwardens' accounts, 1862-1970. 5 fiche. K.F.H.S.R.P. **460**. 1986. Filmed from the original manuscript.

All Saints, Lydd overseers accounts and nomina ledger 1822-1831. [P237/18/1]. 7 fiche. K.F.H.S.R.P. **524**. 1986. Filmed from the original manuscripts.

All Saints, Lydd, overseers assessments ... K.F.H.S.R.P. **523** & **528-9**. 1986. Filmed from the original assessments. Contents: **523**. 1822-6. 5 fiche. **528**. Jan 1834. 1 fiche. **529**. Jul 1834. 1 fiche.

All Saints, Lydd treasurers accts. ... 19 fiche. K.F.H.S.R.P. **513-21**. 1986. Filmed from the original accounts. Contents: **513**. 1926-9. 2 fiche. **514**. 1930-33. 2 fiche. **515**. 1933-37. 2 fiche. **516**. 1937-41. 2 fiche. **517**. 1942-46. 2 fiche. **518**. 1946-52. 2 fiche. **519**. 1952-58. 2 fiche. **520**. 1958-64. 2 fiche. **521**. 1964-71. 3 fiche.

All Saints, Lydd minor church accounts 1922-33. 1 fiche. K.F.H.S.R.P. **525**. 1986. Continued for 1935-61 by **526** (6 fiche). Filmed from the original accounts.

Lydd: London Gazette 3 Aug. 1860 (re tithe). 2 fiche. K.F.H.S.R.P. **527**. 1986. Includes lists of landowners and occupiers.

Lyminge
Ss. M. & E-burge, Lyminge, Vestry minute book 1735-[1855]. 41 fiche. K.F.H.S.R.P. 1481-2. 1988.

Maidstone
CHALKLIN, C.W., ed. *New Maidstone gaol order book, 1805-1823.* Kent records 23. 1984. Many names, mainly of tradesmen, *etc.,* engaged in building the new gaol.

Records of Maidstone, being selection from documents in the possession of the Corporation. Maidstone: Wm. Hobbs & Sons, 1926. Includes lists of the borough records, and of recorders, town clerks, portreeves, and mayors, with many abstracts from the records.

Marden
'Inhabitants of Marden, Kent, 1678', *Home counties magazine* 7, 1905, 307-9. Poor rate assessment.

Morden College
JOYCE, PATRICK. *The history of Morden College, Blackheath, 1695 to the present: patronage and poverty in merchant society.* Henley-on-Thames: Gresham Books, 1982. Includes list of trustees and officers of this almshouse.

Nettlestead
The church wardens accounts of Nettlestead, Kent 1710-1866. 4 fiche. K.F.H.S.R.P. 31. 1984. Filmed from the original accounts.

New Romney
HOLWORTHY, RICHARD. 'The records of New Romney', *Genealogists' magazine* 5, 1929-31, 26-31.

RILEY, HENRY THOMAS. 'Court books of the Corporation of New Romney', in HISTORICAL MANUSCRIPTS COMMISSION. *Sixth report ... Part 1: Report and appendix.* C1745. H.M.S.O., 1877, 540-5.

RILEY, HENRY THOMAS. 'The manuscripts of the Corporation of New Romney', in HISTORICAL MANUSCRIPTS COMMISSION. *Fourth report ... Part 1: Report and appendix.* C857. H.M.S.O., 1874, 439-42.

RILEY, HENRY THOMAS. 'The manuscripts of the Corporation of New Romney', in HISTORICAL MANUSCRIPTS COMMISSION. *Fifth report ... Part 1. Report and appendix.* C.1432. H.M.S.O., 1876, 533-54.

SALISBURY, EDWARD. 'Report on the records of New Romney', *A.C.* 17, 1887, 12-33.

TEICHMAN-DERVILLE, MAJOR. 'The New Romney and Cinque Port records', *A.C.* 42, 1930, 1-36. List.

TEICHMAN-DERVILLE, MAX. *Report and classification of the New Romney records.* Ashford: Headley, 1931. Lists archives of the town.

WALKER, HENRY BACHELOR. 'St. Martin's church, New Romney: records relating to its removal in A.D.1550', *A.C.* 20, 1893, 155-60. Includes accounts, with many names.

Offham
JOHNS, F.D. 'A petty constable's account book', *A.C.* 104, 1988, 9-24. From Offham, 1814-22.

Plumstead
MANDY, W.H. 'Collections for the early history of Plumstead and neighbourhood', *W.D.A.S.A.R.* 21, 1918, 20-21. Abstracts of crown pleas, 1313, *etc.*

MANDY, W.H. 'Plumstead & district in the XIIIth century', *W.D.A.S.A.R.* 20, 1916, 44-56. See also 23, 1926, 25-30. Includes extracts from assize rolls 1255, 1279 and 1293, *etc.*

Queenborough
HULL, FELIX. 'Memoranda from the Queenborough statute book', in HULL, F., ed. *A Kentish miscellany.* Kent records 21, 1979, 79-101. Cover 1452-1556.

FAVRESFELD, CHAS. 'The constables of Queenborough Castle', *Invicta magazine* 3, 1911, 153-64. Includes brief biographical notes on the holders of an important office.

WOODRUFF, C. EVELEIGH. 'Notes on the municipal records of Queenborough, *A.C.* 22, 1897, 169-85.

Rainham
WALTER, JOHN. 'Churchwardens' accounts at Rainham, Kent, A.D.1517-19, and 1565-69', *A.C.* 15, 1883, 333-7.

Ramsgate

K.A.O. catalogues, N.E. Branch, Ramsgate unofficial documents ... 12 fiche. K.F.H.S.R.P. **758-60** 1986. Catalogues of miscellaneous collections.

Rochester

BARTLETT, PHILIP H. *The city of Rochester charters.* Rochester: Rochester City Council, 1961. Includes list of town clerks, 16-20th c.

BECKER, M. JANET. *Rochester Bridge 1387-1856: a history of its early years compiled from the wardens' accounts.* Constable & Co., 1930. Includes a list of account rolls, *etc.*

BLENCOWE, ROBERT WILLIS. 'Rochester records', *A.C.* **2,** 1859, 73-84. Includes transcript of accounts, 1578-80.

BURTT, JOSEPH. 'On the archives of Rochester', *A.C.* **6** 1866, 108-19. Brief discussion.

HARRIS, EDWIN. *The Guildhall, Rochester.* Old Rochester **15.** Rochester: Edwin Harris & Sons, 1900. Lists mayors.

HINKLEY, E.J.F. *A history of the Richard Watts Charity.* Rochester: Richard Watts and the City of Rochester Almshouse Charities, 1979. Includes will of Richard Watts, 1579, lists of officers, *etc.*

L[ARKING], L.B. 'Fabric roll of Rochester Castle', *A.C.* **2,** 1859, 111-32. Accounts, 1367-9.

SCROGGS, E.S. 'The records of Rochester Bridge and of the new college of Cobham', *Archives* **2,** 1953-6, 183-91.

SHEPPARD, J. BRIGSTOCKE. 'The historical mss. belonging to the mayor and corporation of Rochester', in HISTORICAL MANUSCRIPTS COMMISSION. *Ninth report ... Part 1. Report and appendix.* H.M.S.O., 1883, 286-9.

SHEPPARD, J. BRIGSTOCKE. 'The records of the wardens and assistants of Rochester Bridge', in HISTORICAL MANUSCRIPTS COMMISSION. *Ninth report ... Part 1. Report and appendix.* H.M.S.O., 1883, 285-6.

YATES, NIGEL, & GIBSON, JAMES M., eds. *Traffic and politics: the construction and management of Rochester Bridge, A.D.43-1993.* Woodbridge: Boydell Press, 1994. Extensive; includes list of wardens and assistants of Rochester Bridge, 14-20th c.

Romney

MURRAY, K.M. ELISABETH, ed. *Register of Daniel Rough, common clerk of Romney, 1353-1380.* Kent records **16.** 1945.

Saint Margaret at Cliffe

MACFIE, A.L. 'The work of the parish vestry, 1601-1894, St. Margaret's-at-Cliffe', *J.K.L.H.* **20,** 1985, 5-7. General discussion.

Saint Mary Cray

SNELLING, JOSH. ed. 'Ad valorem of the parish of St. Mary Cray, 1831', *N.W.K.F.H.S.* **6**(5), 1993, 156-8. Rating valuation, 1831.

Sandwich

DORMAN, THOMAS. 'The Sandwich book of orphans', *A.C.* **16,** 1886, 179-206. Accounts, 16-17th c.

RILEY, HENRY THOMAS. 'The Corporation of Sandwich', in HISTORICAL MANUSCRIPTS COMMISSION. *Fifth report ... Part 1. Report and appendix.* C1432. H.M.S.O., 1876, 568-71. Description of its archives.

SCROGGS, EDITH S. *A classified list of the records lodged in the Guildhall of the town and port of Sandwich.* Sandwich: Sandwich Corporation, 1932.

Sandwich charters and local government. Rev. ed. Sandwich: Sandwich Local History Society, 1980. General study.

Seal

EATTELL, MADELAINE. *The plight of the poor in the parish of Seal.* Seal and Kensing history publications **3.** [1987?] Includes extracts from original sources.

Seasalter

LUGARD, C.E. *The sess of Seasalter, 1653-1678 with index, 1704-1745 with index, and 1821.* Ashover: C.E. Lugard, 1930.

Selling

NEAME, ALAN. 'The Selling church book, 1778-1845', *K.F.H.S.J.* **5**(10), 1989, 372-6; **5**(12), 1989, 458-60.

The Selling church book 1775-1845. 6 fiche. K.F.H.S.R.P. **1038.** 1987. Filmed from the original manuscripts, with introduction and index by Alan Neame.

NEAME, ALAN. 'The Selling Workhouse 1779-1790', *K.F.H.S.J.* **6**(4), 1990, 127.
NEAME, ALAN. 'The Selling poor book, 1779-1793', *K.F.H.S.J.* **6**(2), 1990, 58.
The Selling poor book 1779-1793. 6 fiche. K.F.H.S.R.P. **1039**. 1987. Filmed from the original manuscript, with introduction and index by Alan Neame.

Sevington
Sevington parish records: churchwardens accounts 1706-1756 (incomplete). 6 fiche. K.F.H.S.R.P. **1077**. 1988. Continued for 1763-1890 in **1078**. (26 fiche)
Sevington parish records: inventory 1953; faculty 1962; proclamation 1799. 2 fiche. K.F.H.S.R.P. **1079**. 1988. Filmed from the original manuscripts.

Shoreham
SAYNOR, JOY. 'The parish administration of Shoreham, 1782-1894', *A.C.* **87**, 1973, 191-203. Based on parochial records.

Shorne
ALLEN, A.F. 'An early Poor Law account', *A.C.* **64**, 1952, 74-84. Includes brief extracts from Shorne accounts, early 17th c.

Sibertswold
Shepherdswell [Sibertswold], Kent, churchwardens' accounts, 1785-1830. 3 fiche. K.F.H.S.R.P. **323**. 1986. For 1832-1917, see **324** (4 fiche). Filmed from the original accounts.
Shepherdswell [Sibertswold], Kent: surveyors accounts, 1805-1836. 2 fiche. K.F.H.S.R.P. **336**. 1986. Filmed from the original accounts.
Shepherdswell [Sibertswold], Kent, vestry minutes 1807-37, & P.C.C. minutes 1911-15. 3 fiche. K.F.H.S.R.P. **325**. 1986. Filmed from the original manuscript. For P.C.C. minutes 1916-23, see **326** (2 fiche); 1923-31, **327** (3 fiche); 1932-7, **328** (2 fiche); 1937-48, **329** (6 fiche). 1947-56, **330** (3 fiche); 1955-62 (including vestry minutes 1918-21), **331**. (4 fiche).
Shepherdswell [Sibertswold], Kent: P.C.C. Correspondence and papers, 1848-1953. 9 fiche. K.F.H.S.R.P. **332**. 1986. Filmed from

the original manuscripts. For further papers, 1910-60, see **333** (6 fiche, also including electoral rolls, 1937, 1938 & 1947) & **334** (6 fiche).
Shepherdswell [Sibertswold], Kent: overseers' accounts, 1807-1934. 6 fiche. K.F.H.S.R.P. **335**. 1986. Filmed from the original accounts.
Shepherdswell [Sibertswold], Kent: Young Men's Club minutes & accounts, 1943-56. 3 fiche. K.F.H.S.R.P. **338**. 1986. Filmed from the original minutes.
Shepherdswell [Sibertswold], Kent: miscellaneous items. Includes glebe terriers, petitions, photographs 3 fiche. K.F.H.S.R.P. **342**. 1986. See also **344**. Filmed from the original manuscripts.
Shepherdswell, Kent: Parochial Church Council accounts, 1934-1946. 3 fiche. K.F.H.S.R.P. **349**. 1986. Filmed from the original accounts.
Shepherdswell. Accts., P.C.C. 1946-51, & church, 1893-1910; subscribers, bills, corres., hist. notes, etc. 3 fiche. K.F.H.S.R.P. **350**. 1986. Filmed from the original manuscripts.

Smarden
HASLEWOOD, FRANCIS. 'Notes from the records of Smarden church', *A.C.* **9**, 1874, 224-35. Extracts from churchwardens' accounts, 1536-1602.

Staplehurst
ELLISTON-ERWOOD, F.C. 'More notes on Kentish roads', *A.C.* **73**, 1960, 167-92. Includes accounts of Staplehurst parish surveyors, 1731-2.

Strood
LOMER, HENRY R. *The churchwardens' accounts of St. Nicholas, Strood.* (B.M. Add. Ms. 36,937). 2 pts. Kent records **5**. 1915-27. Pt.1. 1555-1600. Pt.2. 1603-1662.
SMETHAM, H.Y. 'An old parish account book, Strood', *Kent magazine* **1**(1), 1896 34-44. Brief extracts, 18th c.

Sturry
Assessment records, 1716-1743, made by the churchwardens and overseers of Sturry, Kent. 5 fiche. K.F.H.S.R.P. **223**. [1986?] Filmed from the original manuscript.

Assessment records, 1743-1790, made by the churchwardens and overseers of Sturry, Kent. 5 fiche. K.F.H.S.R.P. **224.** [1986?] Filmed from the original manuscript.

Assessment records, 1790-1843 & 1592, made by the churchwardens and overseers of Sturry, Kent. 7 fiche. K.F.H.S.R.P. **225.** [1986?] Filmed from the original manuscript.

Sturry, Kent. Churchwardens' accounts 1827-71 ... & J.P.'s grants for Navy service 1797. 2 fiche. K.F.H.S.R.P. **250.** 1986. Filmed from the original manuscripts.

Churchwardens' accounts of Sturry, Kent: vouchers, 1834-1870, with gaps. K.F.H.S.R.P. **227.** [1986?] Filmed from the original manuscripts.

Churchwardens' accounts of Sturry, Kent: vouchers, 1831-1870, with gaps. 7 fiche. K.F.H.S.R.P. **228.** [1986?] Filmed from the original manuscript.

Churchwardens' accounts of Sturry, Kent: vouchers 1830-1880, with gaps. 7 fiche. K.F.H.S.R.P. **226.** [1986?] Filmed from the original manuscripts.

Churchwardens' accounts of Sturry, Kent: vouchers 1835-1871 with gaps. 7 fiche. K.F.H.S.R.P. **229.** [1986?] Filmed from the original manuscripts.

Overseers' and churchwardens' nominations at the vestry, Sturry, Kent, 1737-1835, & memoranda. 3 fiche. K.F.H.S.R.P. **230.** [1986?] Filmed from the original manuscript.

Parochial Church Council accounts 1938-1944 & correspondence, of Sturry, Kent. 1 fiche. K.F.H.S.R.P. **235.** 1986. Filmed from the original manuscripts.

Sturry, Kent: P.C.C. Accts., & letters, minutes of committees, 1939-41. 2 fiche. K.F.H.S.R.P. **268.** 1986. Filmed from the original manuscripts.

Vestry minutes of Sturry, Kent, 1836-1917. 5 fiche. K.F.H.S.R.P. **231.** [1986?] Filmed from the original manuscripts.

Vestry and Parochial Church Council minutes of Sturry, Kent 1927-1947. 6 fiche. K.F.H.S.R.P. **232.** 1986. For 1945-58, see **233** (3 fiche); 1956-67, **234** (4 fiche). Filmed from the original manuscripts.

Miscellaneous receipts for the parish of Sturry, Kent, 1948-51. 2 fiche. K.F.H.S.R.P.

248. 1986. For 1939-52 (also including Sunday School accounts 1942-8, and fellowship accounts 1941-5) see **249.** (3 fiche) Filmed from the original manuscripts.

Sturry, Kent, surveyors bills and receipts, 1830-[61]. Fiche. K.F.H.S.R.P. **254-60.** 1986. Filmed from the original bills.

Sturry, Kent: Bigg's Charity records, including leases, 17th-19th century. 4 fiche. K.F.H.S.R.P. **272.** 1986. Filmed from the original manuscripts.

Sturry, Kent: papers & deeds relating to Biggs Charity 1676-1833, & items re Church Hall. 3 fiche. K.F.H.S.R.P. **261.** 1986. Filmed from the original manuscripts.

Sturry, Kent: 5 indentures 1637-1753; mss. 18th cent., hymns, Bank of England receipt 1857-66. 1 fiche. K.F.H.S.R.P. **263.** 1986. Filmed from the original manuscripts.

Sturry apprenticeships, 1616-1823; bastardy, 1635-1826; orders, 1700-1793; examinations 1729-1796, etc. 3 fiche. K.F.H.S.R.P. **252.** 1986. Also includes title deeds, 1596-1637, and 16th c. churchwardens accounts. Filmed from the original manuscripts.

Sturry settlement certs., 1689-1830; removal orders 1676-1829; bastardy 1817-28; examinations, &c. 12 fiche. K.F.H.S.R.P. **251.** 1986. Filmed from the original manuscripts.

Sturry special committees mins. & accts: bellringers 1923-59; finance 1940-1968; friends 1948-1964. 8 fiche. K.F.H.S.R.P. **271.** 1986. Filmed from the original manuscripts.

Sturry P.C.C. petty cash book no. 1, 1942-1945. 3 fiche. K.F.H.S.R.P. **1081.** 1988. Filmed from the original manuscript.

See also Westbere

Swalecliffe

BOWDEN, C. *Swalecliffe churchwardens accounts 1711-1844.* 5 fiche. K.F.H.S.R.P. **1638.** 1991.

Tenterden

RILEY, HENRY THOMAS. 'The Corporation of Tenterden', in HISTORICAL MANUSCRIPTS COMMISSION. *Sixth report ... Part 1: Report and appendix.* C1745. H.M.S.O., 1877, 569-72. Report on archives.

TAYLOR, A.H. 'The municipal records of Tenterden', *A.C.* **32**, 1917, 283-302; **33**, 1918, 91-112.

Tonbridge
DUMBRECK, W.V. 'The Lowy of Tonbridge', *A.C.* **72**, 1958, 138-47. Extracts from two 13th c., perambulations, giving names of jurors, tenants, *etc.*

WILMOT, E.P. 'Poverty, charity and disease in Tonbridge parish 1650-1750', *J.K.L.H.* **23**, 1986, 9-10. Includes extracts from overseers' accounts, 1671-1729.

Ulcombe
PANTON, F.H. 'Ulcombe poor in the late eighteenth-early nineteenth century', *A.C.* **110**, 1993, 139-51. Includes accounts for 1821, listing payments made to paupers; also various extracts from vestry book.

Westbere
Westbere parish apprenticeship, militia and miscellaneous. 5 fiche. K.F.H.S.R.P. **937**. [198-?] Filmed from the original manuscript.

Westbere parish overseers' accounts, 1663-[1867]. 28 fiche. K.F.H.S.R.P. **930-936**. [198-?] Filmed from the original manuscripts.

COTON, BETTY. *Poor law and order: Westbere and Sturry, 1700-1750. (with special reference to children).* 2 fiche. K.F.H.S.R.P. **1036**. 1987. Thesis; includes some documents.

Westbere parish records: churchwardens' accounts 1695-1728. 25 fiche. K.F.H.S.R.P. **914**. [198-]. Filmed from the original accounts. Continued by:
915. 1728-64.
916. 1765-1840.
917. 1840-1913.
918. 1900-1914.
919. 1914-31.
920. 1938-48.

Westbere parish vestry minutes 1870-1926. 3 fiche. K.F.H.S.R.P. **927**. [198-?]

Westbere parish P.C.C. minutes 1920-33. 2 fiche. K.F.H.S.R.P. **928**. [198-?]. Continued for 1933-58 in **929**.

Westbere P.C.C. accounts 1949-1951. 1 fiche. K.F.H.S.R.P. **921**. [198-?] Filmed from the original accounts.

Westbere parish property, correspondence and accounts. 2 fiche. K.F.H.S.R.P. **926**. [198-?] See also **924**.

Wilmington
STRINGER, SAM. 'Wilmington parochial charities', *Dartford Historical & Antiquarian Society newsletter* **30**, 1993, 4-12. General discussion of each charity.

Wigham
AITKEN, KENNETH G. 'The churchwardens of the parish of Wingham 1720-1860', *K.F.H.S.J.* **5**(8), 1988, 291-3. Includes list.

Wood
See Birchington

Wye
HUNNISET, R.F., ed. 'A coroners' roll of the liberty of Wye', in HUNNISET, R.F., & POST, J.B., eds. *Medieval legal records edited in memory of C.A.F. Meekings.* H.M.S.O., 1978, 130-41. For 1314.

KEITH-LUCAS, B. 'Wye charities for the relief of the poor', *Wye local history* **4**(3), 1984, 8-12. Includes notes on benefactors.

11. CHURCH RECORDS

A. Church of England

The role of the church in pre-industrial society was much wider than it is today. Consequently, many of the records essential to the genealogist are to be found in ecclesiastical rather than state archives — for example, parish registers and records, probate records, marriage licences, *etc.* Works on church records are listed throughout this bibliography; this section concentrates on those records primarily concerned with the administration and life of the church. These records are particularly useful to those with clergy ancestors.

A number of works provide surveys of churches in the county:

GRAYLING, FRANCIS. *Kent.* County churches series. 2 vols. George Allen & Company, 1913.

GLYNNE, STEPHEN R., SIR. *Notes on the churches of Kent.* John Murray, 1877. Mainly architectural description.

HUSSEY, ARTHUR. *Notes on the churches in the counties of Kent, Sussex and Surrey mentioned in the Domesday Book, and those of more recent date, including comparative lists of the churches, and some account of the sepulchral memorials and other antiquities.* John Russell Smith, 1852. Includes brief notes on 360 Kentish churches.

OYLER, THOMAS H. *The parish churches of the Diocese of Canterbury with descriptive notes.* Hurter and Longhurst, 1910.

SYMS, JAMES ANTONY. *Kent county churches: a personal exploration.* Hadlow: J.A. Syms, 1984. Sketches of each church, with brief historical accounts.

SYMS, JAMES ANTONY. *Kent county churches continued.* Rainham: Meresborough Books, 1987.

SYMS, JAMES ANTONY. *Kent county churches concluded.* Rainham: Meresborough Books, 1989.

More specific works on this topic include:

DUNCAN, LELAND L. 'The parish churches of West Kent: their dedications, altars, images and lights', *Transactions of the St. Pauls Ecclesiological Society* 3, 1895, 241-98. Includes many extracts from wills.

HUSSEY, ARTHUR. 'Chapels in Kent', *A.C.* 29, 1911, 217-67. Attempts to identify medieval chapels; gives names of many benefactors and clergy. Also identifies hospitals.

HOMAN, ROGER. *The Victorian churches of Kent.* Chichester: Phillimore & Co., 1984. Inter-denominational. Includes a detailed gazetteer; also a list of architects.

For chantries, see:

HUSSEY, ARTHUR. *Kent chantries.* Kent records 12. 1936. Brief accounts of the history of each chantry, including names of priests, and abstracts of chantry certificates of 1546 and 1548.

Supplemented by:

HOLLAND, EDWARD LANCELOT. *The Canterbury chantries and hospitals, together with some others in the neighbourhood in 1546; a supplement to 'Kent chantries',* ed. Charles Colton. Kent records 12, supplement. 1934.

HUSSEY, ARTHUR. *Kent obit and lamp rents.* Kent records 14. 1936. Based on the chantry certificates of 1548.

Studies of church bells and plate may yield valuable genealogical information. See:

STAHLSCHMIDT, J.C.L. *The church bells of Kent: their inscriptions, founders, uses and traditions.* Elliot Stock, 1887. Includes various extracts from churchwardens' accounts, as well as noting numerous inscriptions giving names of benefactors, clergy, churchwardens, *etc.*

ROBERTSON, W.A. SCOTT. 'Church plate in Kent', *A.C.* 16, 1886, 327-439; 17, 1887, 241-320. Includes list of donors, 1485-1761.

Continued by:

WOODRUFF, C.E. 'Church plate in Kent', *A.C.* 25, 1902, 113-97; 26, 1904, 136-266; 27, 1905, 262-300; 28, 1909, 115-55.

A number of works on Kentish monasteries are available; these may provide the names of monks, benefactors, officers, *etc.* For their estate records, see above, section 8B. A brief bibliography of Kentish monasteries is printed in:

BURRIDGE, DAVID, 'Monastic Kent: a bibliography', *B.K.* 3(1), 1992, 37-40.
The county of Kent was divided ecclesiastically into the dioceses of Canterbury and Rochester. There was only one archdeaconry in each diocese; with the exception of a number of 'peculiars' in Rochester diocese, (especially Shoreham Deanery) the jurisdiction of the Archdeaconry courts was concurrent with that of the Consistory courts. Most works on the Church of England in Kent are confined to one of the dioceses, and are, therefore, listed here separately. For the records of the Province of Canterbury - especially the Prerogative Court of Canterbury - see Raymond's *English genealogy: a bibliography.*

Canterbury Diocese
For a general history of the diocese, see:
JENKINS, ROBERT C. *Canterbury.* Diocesan histories. Society for Promoting Christian Knowledge, 1880.
There are many works on the Archbishops. See, for example:
CARPENTER, EDWARD. *Cantuar: the Archbishops in their office.* Cassell, 1971. A study of their activities.
HOOK, WALTER FARQUHAR. *Lives of the Archbishops of Canterbury.* 2nd ed. 11 vols. Richard Bentley, 1861-75. To be used with considerable discretion.
MCKILLIAM, A.E. *A chronicle of the Archbishops of Canterbury.* James Clarke & Co., 1913.
Archbishops, archdeacons and priors are listed in:
LE NEVE, JOHN. *Fasti ecclesiae Anglicanae, 1066-1300, II: monastic cathedrals (Northern and Southern Provinces),* compiled by Diana E. Greenway. Athlone Press, 1971. A further volume covering 1300-1541, compiled by B.Jones, was published in 1963.
LE NEVE, JOHN. *Fasti ecclesiae Anglicanae, 1541-1857, III: Canterbury, Rochester and Winchester dioceses,* compiled by Joyce M. Horn. Athlone Press, 1974.
The archives of the Archdiocese of Canterbury are, of course, of relevance to the whole of Southern England, not just

Kent. Useful background information on them may be found in:
CHURCHILL, I.J., et al. *Medieval records of the Archbishops of Canterbury: a course of public lectures delivered in Lambeth Palace Library in 1960.* Faith Press, 1962. Includes chapters on 'The Archbishops' register', by Irene J. Churchill, and 'The Archbishop's testamentary jurisdiction', by E.F. Jacob, *etc.*
For the archives of the Diocese of Canterbury, see:
Catalogue of records of the Diocese of Canterbury deposited in the Cathedral Library. 3 fiche. K.F.H.S.R.P. **965.** [198-?]
Of more specifically Kentish interest are:
WOODRUFF, C. EVELEIGH. 'The records of the courts of the Archdeaconry and Consistory of Canterbury', *A.C.* **41,** 1929, 89-105. List, with some extracts.
WOODCOCK, BRIAN LINDSAY. *Medieval ecclesiastical courts in the Diocese of Canterbury.* Oxford University Press, 1952. Includes lists of officers of the courts, and a bibliography.

Medieval Acta and Bishops' Registers
CHENEY, C.R., &. JONES, BRIDGETT E.A., eds. *English episcopal acta II: Canterbury, 1162-1190.* Oxford: Oxford University Press, for the British Academy, 1986.
CHENEY, C.R., & JOHN, ERIC, *English episcopal acta III: Canterbury 1193-1205.* Oxford: Oxford University Press, for the British Academy, 1986.
The registers of the Archbishop of Canterbury 13th-17th centuries. 20 microfilm reels. World Microfilms, [1995?]
MAJOR, KATHLEEN, ed. *Acta Stephani Langton, Cantuariensis archiepiscopi, A.D. 1207-1228.* Canterbury and York Society **50.** 1950.
DAVIS, F.N., ed. *The register of John Pecham, Archbishop of Canterbury, 1279-1292.* Canterbury and York Society **63 & 65.** 1968-9.
MARTIN, CHARLES TRICE. *Registrum epistolarum fratris Johannis Peckham, Archiepiscopi Cantuarienses.* (1279-92.) 3 vols. Rolls series. Longman & Co., 1882-5.

MAJOR, KATHLEEN, ed. *Registrum Roberti Winchelsey, Cantuariensis archiepiscopi, A.D.1294-1313.* 2 vols. Canterbury and York Society **51-2.** 1952-6.

WOOD, A.C., ed. *Registrum Simonis de Langham, Cantuariensis archiepiscopi.* Canterbury and York Society **53.** 1956. For 1366-8.

JACOB, E.F., ed. *The register of Henry Chichele, Archbishop of Canterbury 1414-1443.* Oxford: Clarendon Press, 1938-47. Also published as Canterbury and York Society, **42-7.**

DU BOULAY, F.R.H., ed. *Registrum Thome Bourgchier, Cantuariensis archiepiscopi, A.D. 1454-1486.* Canterbury and York Society **54.** 1957.

FRERE, W.H., ed. *Registrum Matthei Parker, diocesis Cantuariensis, A.D. 1559-1575,* transcribed by E.Margaret Thompson, ed. W.H.Frere. 3 vols. Canterbury and York Society **35-6 & 39.** 1928-33.

Act Books

WOODRUFF, C. EVELEIGH. 'Notes from a fourteenth century act-book of the Consistory Court of Canterbury', *A.C.* **40,** 1928, 53-64. Extracts.

WILLIS, ARTHUR J. *Calendar of the extant act books of detecta in the Diocese of Canterbury 1559-1565.* 7 fiche. K.F.H.S.R.P. **160.** 1985.

Archdeaconry Ct. of Canterbury instance act books. 136 fiche. K.F.H.S.R.P. **1496-9.** 1988. Filmed from the original manuscripts. Contents:
1496. 1719-1760
1497. 1639-1640
1498. 1640-1641
1499. 1641-1661.

DUNKIN, E.H.W., et al. *Index to the act books of the Archbishops of Canterbury 1663-1859.* 2 vols. Index library **55 & 63.** British Record Society, 1929-38. For the whole Province.

Deposition Registers

Archdeaconry Ct. of Canterbury deposition register. 726 fiche. K.F.H.S.R.P. **1500-1519.** 1988. Covers 1555-98. Filmed from the original register.

Archdeaconry Court of Canterbury depositions register PRC 39/24 1599-1602. 7 fiche. K.F.H.S.R.P. **1035.** [198-?]

Consistory Court deposition registers 1662-1682. 36 fiche. K.F.H.S.R.P. **1495.** 1988. Filmed from the original registers.

Presentations and Institutions

WOODRUFF, C. EVELEIGH, ed. *Calendar of institutions by the Chapter of Canterbury sede vacante.* Kent records **8.** 1923. For the Province of Canterbury.

See also the bishops registers, above.

Inventories of Church Goods

WALCOTT, MACKENZIE E.C. 'Inventories of parish church goods in Kent, A.D. 1552', *A.C.* **8,** 1872, 74-163; **9,** 1874, 266-84, **10,** 1876, 282-97; **11,** 1877, 409-16. Includes names of clergy, churchwardens, *etc.* Continued in:

ROBERTSON, W.A. SCOTT. 'Inventories of parish church goods in Kent, A.D. 1552', *A.C.* **14,** 1882, 290-312.

'Queen Mary's responsibility for parish church goods seized by King Edward's commissioners', *A.C.* **14,** 1882, 313-25. Accounts shewing how they were disposed of; includes names of purchasers of Canterbury goods.

Licences

WILLIS, ARTHUR J. *Canterbury licences (general) 1568-1646.* Chichester: Phillimore, 1972. Includes licences for schoolmasters, physicians, midwives, parish clerks, curates, preachers, *etc.,* also a few marriage licences not published in Cowper's *Canterbury marriage licences* (see vol. 2 of this bibliography)

Visitation Records

WOODRUFF, C. EVELEIGH. 'Some early visitation rolls preserved at Canterbury', *A.C.* **32,** 1917, 143-80; **33,** 1918, 71-90. 13-14th c.

WOODRUFF, C. EVELEIGH. 'An archidiaconal visitation of 1502', *A.C.* **47,** 1935, 13-54. Many names of clergy, churchwardens, *etc.*

WOOD-LEGH, K.L., ed. *Kentish visitation of Archbishop William Warham and his deputies, 1511-1512.* Kent records **24.** 1984.

WHATMORE, L.E., ed. *Archdeacon Harpsfield's visitation, 1557*. 2 vols. Publications of the Catholic Record Society, **45-6**. 1950-51.

JENKINS, CLAUDE. 'An unpublished record of Archbishop Parker's visitation in 1573', *A.C.* **29**, 1911, 270-318. Presentments.

Other Records

FRAMPTON, T.S. 'Early presentations to Kentish benefices', *A.C.* **20**, 1893, 64-70. For 1199-1216.

WOODRUFF, C. EVELEIGH. 'Some early professions of Canonical obedience to the See of Canterbury, by heads of religious houses', *A.C.* **37**, 1925, 53-72. Includes lists of the abbots of Boxley, Canterbury, Faversham, Langdon, *etc.*, with notes, 12-13th c.

K.A.O. *Probate catalogue PRC 43 and PRC 44*. 1 fiche. K.F.H.S.R.P. **711**. 1986. The title of this fiche is a misnomer; it actually lists various ecclesiastical records, including a return of communicants and householders in the Diocese of Canterbury, 1565, and records of court proceedings.

LAMBARDE, E. 'Some Kentish charities, 1594', *A.C.* **31**, 1915, 189-202. Abstracts of presentments relating to various charities, including names of benefactors, *etc.*

WOODRUFF, C. EVELEIGH. 'Extracts from original documents illustrating the progress of the Reformation in Kent', *A.C.* **40**, 1915, 92-120.

DUNCAN, LELAND L. 'The renunciation of the Papal authority by the clergy of West Kent, 1534', *A.C.* **22**, 1897, 293-309. Transcript of a declaration denying the authority of the Pope, with signatures of (and brief notes on) the local clergy.

BUCKINGHAM, C. 'The movement of clergy in the Diocese of Canterbury, 1552-62', *Recusant history* **14**, 1978, 219-41.

WILLIS, ARTHUR J. *Church life in Kent, being church court records of the Canterbury Diocese, 1559-1565*. Chichester: Phillimore, 1975.

WOODRUFF, C. EVELEIGH. 'Letters relating to the condition of the church in Kent during the Primacy of Archbishop Sancroft [1678-1690]', *A.C.* **21**, 1895, 172-97. Includes brief notes on churches in the jurisdiction of the Archdeacon of Canterbury — including character sketches of clergy.

The Canterbury diocesan clergy list, church calendar and general almanack. Church Press, 1869- . Title varies.

Diocese of Rochester

The Diocese of Rochester has attracted much less attention from historians than Canterbury, and few diocesan sources are in print. For a general history, see:

PEARMAN, A.I. *Rochester*. Diocesan histories. Society for Promoting Christian Knowledge, 1897.

For the archives of the Diocese, see:

K.A.O. *unofficial document catalogue: Rochester Diocesan catalogue*. 4 fiche. K.F.H.S.R.P. **707**. 1986.

The archives of the Dean & Chapter of Rochester, c.1100-1907. 43 fiche. K.F.H.S.R.P. **684-9**. 1986. Filmed from a hand-written calendar.

The archives of the Dean and Chapter of Rochester, c.1100-1907. Brief guide to the catalogue. 3 fiche. K.F.H.S.R.P. **710**. 1986.

An early bishop's register, including a list of ordinations, and the bishop's will, is printed in:

JOHNSON, CHARLES, ed. *Registrum Hamonis Hethe, Diocesis Roffensis, A.D.1319-1352*. 2 vols. Kent records **4**. 1915-48. Vol. 2 includes an extensive list of ordinands. Also published as Canterbury and York Society **48-9**, 1948.

For a brief transcript of 14th c. court proceedings, see:

PARKER, SANDRA LEE, & POOS, LAWRENCE R. 'A consistory court from the Diocese of Rochester 1363-1364', *English historical review* **106**, 1991, 652-65.

Brief biographies of the bishops of Rochester are contained in:

HARRIS, EDWIN. *Bishops of Rochester, A.D.604-1897*. Old Rochester **4**. Rochester: MacKays, 1897.

For diocesan officials, see Le Neve's *Fasti ecclesiae Anglicanae ...*, cited above under Canterbury Diocese. Two separately published lists of diocesan officials are also available:

ARNOLD, A.A. 'The Chancellors of the Diocese of Rochester', *A.C.* **24**,. 1900, 160-74. List, with biographical notes.

BROWNE, A.L. 'The medieval officials — principal of Rochester', *A.C.* **53**, 1941, 29-61. Includes biographical notes.

The clergy of the diocese are listed in:

FIELDING, C.H. *The records of Rochester.* Dartford: Snowden Brothers, 1910. This also includes notes on individual churches.

Adisham

ROBERTSON, W.A. SCOTT. 'Forty rectors of Adisham', *A.C.* **14**, 1882, 162-8. Includes biographical notes.

Bethersden

PEARMAN, A.J. 'Bethersden: its church and monumental inscriptions', *A.C.* **16**, 1886, 66-98. Includes list of vicars, with biographical notes; also extracts from registers, and various monumental inscriptions, with pedigrees of Hulse 17th c., Dyne, 17-19th c., Witherden, 16-19th c., Whitfield, 17-19th c., Wilmott, 17-19th c., and Gibbon, 16th c.

Bexley

ROBERTSON, W.A. SCOTT. 'Bexley: the church; Hall Place; and Blendon', *A.C.* **18**, 1889, 369-82. Includes list of vicars, with biographical notes; also descents of Hall Place and Blendon.

Birchington

All Saints, Birchington. Church repairs accts. 18th & 19th cent. 3 fiche. K.F.H.S.R.P. **540**. 1986. Filmed from the original manuscripts.

All Saints, Birchington church restoration documents 1864. 1 fiche. K.F.H.S.R.P. **545**. 1986. Includes list of subscribers.

Bexley

TESTER, P.J. 'Lost eighteenth-century charity books formerly in St. Mary's church, Bexley', *A.C.* **96**, 1981, 391-4. See also **101**, 1985, 358. Transcript of inscription, naming benefactors; includes notes.

Blackheath Hundred

BAKER, L.A.J. *Churches in the Hundred of Blackheath: a list of the places of worship in the boroughs of Deptford, Greenwich, Lewisham, and Woolwich, under each of which is listed the books or pamphlets dealing with the history of the church and its ministers.* Greenwich: Greenwich and Lewisham Antiquarian Society, 1961.

CARNEGIE, MOIR. 'Church plate in the Hundred of Blackheath', *T.G.L.A.S.* **4**(2), 1939, 63-111. Inclues many names of donors and makers.

Boxley Abbey

FIELDING, C.H. 'Boxley Abbey', *Invicta magazine* **3**, 1911, 139-49. Includes list of abbots.

Bredgar

PARKING, E.W. 'The old chantry house, Bredgar', *A.C.* **91**, 1976, 87-97. Includes list of priests, *etc.,* 1393-1532.

Broadstairs

LAPTHORNE, W.H. 'Chronology of incumbents of Holy Trinity, Broadstairs', *B.K.* **15**(1), 1994, 47-50. 19-20th c.

Canterbury

'Canterbury parish churches, 13th to 17th century', K.F.H.S.N. **6**(5), 1990, 159-60. Chronology of openings and closings (etc.

Cathedral

Many works are devoted to the history of Canterbury Cathedral, and only a small selection can be listed here. Works relating to the estates of the cathedral priory are listed above, section 8. For general histories, see:

COLLINSON, PATRICK, RAMSAY, NIGEL, & SPARKS, MARGARET, eds. *A history of Canterbury Cathedral.* Oxford: Oxford University Press, 1995. Collection of authoritative articles, including studies of the monuments, and of the Cathedral archives.

WARNER, S.A. *Canterbury Cathedral.* Society for Promoting Christian Knowledge, 1923.

WOODRUFF, C. EVELEIGH, & DANKS, WILLIAM. *Memorials of the Cathedral and Priory of Christ in Canterbury.* Chapman and Hall, 1912. General historical account, including lists of deans, canons and organists, *etc.*

A number of early records have been printed:

CROSS, FRANCIS W. 'The early minute books of the Dean and Chapter of Canterbury', *Archaeological journal* **53**, 1896, 235-48. 16-17th c.

FLEMING, ROBIN. 'Christchurch's sisters and brothers: an edition and discussion of Canterbury obituary lists', in MEYER, MARC ANTHONY, ed. *The culture of Christendom: essays in medieval history in commemoration of Dennis L.T. Bethell.* Cambridge: C.U.P., 1992, 115-53.

GARDINER, DOROTHY. 'Recent discoveries in the archives of Canterbury Cathedral: notes on the monks and Priory buildings mentioned', *A.C.* **58**, 1946, 40-42.

WOODRUFF, C. EVELEIGH. 'The sacrist's rolls of Christ Church, Canterbury', *A.C.* **48**, 1936, 38-80. Accounts, 14-15th c., includes list of sacrists.

LEGG, J. WICKHAM, & HOPE, W.H. ST. JOHN. *Inventories of Christ Church, Canterbury, with historical and illustrative documents.* Archibald Constable & Co., 1902. Many names.

Numerous medieval letters are printed in two works:

SHEPPARD, R. BRIGSTOCKE, ed. *Literae Cantuarienses: the letter books of the monastery of Christ Church, Canterbury.* 3 vols. Rolls series **85**. 1887-9.

SHEPPARD, J.B., ed. *Christ Church letters: a volume of medieval letters relating to the affairs of the Priory of Christ Church, Canterbury.* Camden Society N.S., **19**. 1877.

Two medieval chronicles of Christ Church have been published:

SEARLE, WILLIAM GEORGE, ed. *Christ Church, Canterbury. I: The chronicle of John Stone, monk of Christ Church, 1415-1471. II: Lists of the Deans, Priors and monks of Christ Church monastery.* Cambridge Antiquarian Society Octavo publications **34**. 1902.

WOODRUFF, C. EVELEIGH. 'The chronicle of William Glastynbury, monk of the Priory of Christ Church, Canterbury, 1419-1448', *A.C.* **37**, 1925, 121-51. Includes a list of the officers of Christ Church Priory, Canterbury, in 1435, *etc.*

A number of biographical works are devoted to the Deans:

COWPER J. MEADOWS. *The lives of the deans of Canterbury, 1541-1900.* Canterbury: Cross & Jackman, 1900.

TODD, HENRY JOHN. *Some account of the Deans of Canterbury from the new foundation of that church by Henry the Eighth to the present time, to which is added a catalogue of the manuscripts in the church library.* Canterbury: Simms and Kirkby and Jones, 1793.

STRONG, ROY. 'Portraits of the Deans of Canterbury in the Deanery', *Canterbury Cathedral chronicle* **65**, 1970, 102-11. List of 32 portraits.

For brief biographies of the Six Preachers, see:

HILL, DEREK INGRAM. *The six preachers of Canterbury Cathedral, 1542-1982: clerical lives from Tudor times to the present day.* Ramsgate: K.H. McIntosh, 1982.

See also:

WOODRUFF, C. EVELEIGH. *A list of the six preachers of the cathedral and metropolitan Church of Christ in Canterbury.* Canterbury: Gibbs and Sons, 1926. 1541-1919.

Other works include:

HATCHER, J. 'Mortality in the fifteenth century: some new evidence', *Economic history review* 2nd series **39**, 1986, 19-38. Based on the obituary lists of Christ Church Priory, Canterbury.

W., C.E. 'Canterbury Cathedral: a contemporary list of the members of King Henry VIIIth's new foundation', *Canterbury Cathedral chronicle* **37**, 1941, 9-13. 1541.

Grey Friars

COTTON, CHARLES. *The Grey Friars of Canterbury, 1224 to 1538: a contribution to the 700th anniversary of their arrival in England.* British Society of Franciscan Studies, extra series **2**. Manchester: the

University Press, 1924. Includes list of wardens and friars, with extracts from benefactors' wills, *etc*

COTTON, CHARLES. 'Notes on the documents in the cathedral library at Canterbury relating to the Grey Friars', in KINGSFORD, C.L., et al, eds. *Collectanea Franciscana II.* British Society of Franciscan Studies **10.** 1922. Brief calendar of letters and papers.

Saint Augustines Abbey
COTTON, CHARLES. 'St. Austin's Abbey, Canterbury: treasurers' accounts 1468-9 and others', *A.C.* **51,** 1940, 66-109.

Cheriton
ROBERTSON, W.A. SCOTT. 'Cheriton church', *A.C.* **18,** 1889, 353-68. Includes list of rectors, with biographical notes.

Chevening
ROBERTSON, W.A. SCOTT. 'Chevening church', *A.C.* **16,** 1886, 114-26. Includes list of rectors, with biographical notes.

Cliffe
LLOYD, IORWERTH GREY. 'Notices of Clyffe-at-Hoo', *A.C.* **15,** 1883, 259-72. Extracts from the registers of the see of Canterbury, 1288-1739, with additions from the parish register.

ROBERTSON, W.A.SCOTT. 'The rectors of Cliffe at Hoo', *A.C.* **15,** 1883, 217-54. Includes biographical notes.

Cowden
DUNCAN, LELAND L. 'The rectory of Cowden', *A.C.* **21,** 1895, 87-94. Lists rectors, with brief biographical notes.

Cranbrook
COLLINSON, PATRICK. 'Cranbrook and the Fletchers: popular and unpopular religion in the Kentish Weald', in his *Godly people: essays in English puritanism and protestantism.* Hambledon Press, 1983, 399-428.

TARBUTT, WILLIAM. *The annals of Cranbrook church, its monuments, ministers and people.* Cranbrook: Mrs. Dennett, 1875.

Dartford
LANDALE, JOHN. *A collection and abstract of all the material deeds, wills, leases, and legal documents relating to the several donations and benefactions to the church and poor of the parish of Dartford in Kent ...* John Hearne, 1829.

ROBERTSON, W.A. SCOTT. 'Dartford church (Holy Trinity)', *A.C.* **18,** 1889, 383-98. Includes list of vicars, with biographical notes.

Davington
COLLIER, CARUS VALE. 'Incumbents of Davington church', *A.C.* **22,** 1897, 289-92.

Deal
STEBBING, W.P.D. 'Briefs in St. Leonards and St. George's parishes in Deal in the seventeenth and eighteenth centuries', *A.C.* **57,** 1945, 26-33. Includes names of some contributors.

Dover
ROBERTSON, W.A. SCOTT. 'The old church of St. Martin at Dover', *A.C.* **20,** 1893, 295-304. Includes list of rectors *etc.* 1302-1468/9.

FIELDING, C.H. 'Dover Priory', *Invicta magazine* **3,** 1913, 11-24. Includes notes on priors.

Eastchurch
ROBERTSON, W.A. SCOTT. 'Vicars of Eastchurch', *A.C.* **14,** 1882, 285-8. List, with biographical notes.

Elham
Elham, Kent, sacrament money acount book for the years 1827-1879. 3 fiche. K.F.H.S.R.P. **310.** 1986. Filmed from the original manuscript.

Eltham Palace
PRAGNELL, H.J. 'Eltham Palace: its chapels and chaplains', *A.C.* **83,** 1969, 205-16. Includes list of chaplains, 1326-1553.

Faversham
GIRAUD, F.W. 'On goods and ornaments at Faversham church, A.D.1512', *A.C.* **18,** 1889, 103-13. Includes biographical notes on donors.

GIRAUD, F.F. 'On the parish clerks and sexton of Faversham, A.D.1506-1593', *A.C.* 20, 1893, 203-10. Includes some names. 'Anchorites in Faversham churchyard', *A.C.* 11, 1877, 24-39. Medieval.

Godmersham

TATTON-BROWN, TIM. 'The parish church of St. Laurence, Godmersham: a history', *A.C.* 106, 1989, 45-81. Mentions many names connected with the church.

Gravesend

HISCOCK, R.H. 'Some notes on the bells of St. George's church, Gravesend', *A.C.* 102, 1986, 27-41. Includes inscriptions on the bells, and the names of various other parishioners.

Greenwich

KIMBELL, JOHN. *An account of the legacies, gifts, rents, fees, &c., appertaining to the church and poor of St. Alphege, Greenwich, in the County of Kent.* Greenwich: G. Allen, 1816.

SHARP, ARTHUR. 'Saint Alfege', *T.G.L.A.S.* 4(1), 1936, 6-28. Greenwich parish church. Includes biographical notes on medieval rectors.

MARTIN, A.R. 'The Grey Friars of Greenwich', *Archaeological journal* 80, 1923, 81-114. Includes extracts from wills relating to the friars, 1482-1534.

High Halden

GRIMALDI, W.B., ed. *Extracts from registers and records relating to the collation, institution, induction and composition of the rectors of High Halden, from A.D. 1322 to 1899.* Privately printed, 1900.

Ickham

FRAMPTON, T. SHIPDEM. 'The chantry of John Denys in Ickham church', *A.C.* 25, 1902, 207-21. Includes biographical notes on charity priests.

ROBERTSON, W.A. SCOTT. 'Ickham church, its monuments and its rectors', *A.C.* 14, 1882, 113-33. Includes pedigrees of Head and Barrett, 17-19th c., and notes on a few inscriptions, but primarily a list of rectors with biographical notes.

Lesnes Abbey

CLAPHAM, ALFRED W. 'The foundation of Lesnes Abbey', *W.D.A.S.A.R.* 15, 1910, 103-38. See also 16, 1911, 49-53. Includes list of abbots, priors and sub-priors, 12-16th c., with pedigree of De Lucy.

FIELDING, C.H. 'Lesness Abbey', *Invicta magazine* 1, 1908, 297-307. Includes list of abbots, *etc.*

Lewisham

DUNCAN, LELAND LEWIS. *The parish church of Saint Mary, Lewisham, Kent: its building and rebuilding, with some account of the vicars and curates of Lewisham.* Lewisham Antiquarian Society, 1892.

MARTIN, A.R. 'The alien priory of Lewisham', *T.G.L.A.S.* 3(3), 1927, 103-26. Includes biographical notes on priors.

Lullingstone

ROBERTSON, W.A. SCOTT. 'Church of St. Botolph, Lullingstone', *A.C.* 16, 1886, 99-113. Includes list of rectors.

Lydd

'Church of All Saints, Lydd', *A.C.* 13, 1880, 427-50. Includes list of clergy, notes relating to the church from the wills of parishioners, pedigree of Dering, 18th c.

Lymne

ROBERTSON, W.A. SCOTT. 'Lymne castle and church', *A.C.* 18, 1889, 436-46. Includes list of vicars, with biographical notes.

Maidstone

CAVE-BROWNE, JOHN. *History of the parish of All Saints, Maidstone.* Maidstone: G. Bunyard, 1889. Includes much information on clergy, and many notes on inscriptions.

POSTE, BEALE. *The history of the College of All Saints, Maidstone.* Maidstone: J. Smith; London: Whittaker and Co., 1847. This was an ecclesiastical establishment rather than a school. Includes many extracts from deeds *etc.*

Milton next Sittingbourne

'Milton subscription to St. Paul's Cathedral', *A.C.* 24, 1900, 225-6. Lists subscribers from Milton; undated, but probably 1630's.

Minster in Sheppey

BRAMSTON, WILLIAM. *History of the Abbey church of Minster, Isle of Sheppey, Kent, with a description of the monuments and other matters relating to this ancient parish.* Hazell, Watson & Viney, 1896. Includes extensive list of subscribers to the restoration fund, late 19th c.

Minster in Thanet

FRAMPTON, T. SHIPDEM. 'St. Mary's church, Minster, Isle of Thanet: list of vicars, *A.C.* **25**, 1902, 97-112. 13-19th c.

New Romney

BUTCHER, A.F. 'The hospital of St. Stephen and St. Thomas, New Romney: the documentary evidence', *A.C.* **96**, 1981, 17-26. Includes list of wardens, 14-15th c.

Orpington

ROBERTSON, W.A. SCOTT. 'Orpington church', *A.C.* **13**, 1880, 374-85. Includes list of clergy, brief notes on monuments, *etc.*

Ospringe

DRAKE, CHARLES H. 'The Hospital of St. Mary of Ospringe, commonly called Maison Dieu', *A.C.* **30**, 1914, 35-78. Includes lists of masters or wardens, 1234-1514, and chantry priests, 1525-44, with deed abstracts, *etc.*

Otham

CAVE-BROWNE, J. 'Otham rectors', *A.C.* **23**, 1898, 184-93.

Patrixbourne

ROBERTSON, W.A. SCOTT. 'Patricksbourne church, and Bifrons', *A.C.* **14**, 1882, 169-84. Includes list of vicars, with biographical notes; also a few notes on inscriptions *etc.* Bifrons is a mansion in the parish.

Pevington

HASLEWOOD, FRANCIS. 'Pevington and its rectors', *A.C.* **22**, 2897, 109-11. List, 1316-1584.

Pluckley

HASLEWOOD, FRANCIS. 'The rectors of Pluckley, Kent, for upwards of six hundred years', *A.C.* **22**, 1897, 85-101. With biographical notes; also pedigree of Selwyn, 17-19th c.

Preston

ROBERTSON, W.A. SCOTT. 'Rectors of Preston-by-Faversham', *A.C.* **21**, 1895, 135-6. 13-14th c.

ROBERTSON, W.A. SCOTT. 'Vicars of Preston-by-Faversham', *A.C.* **21**, 1895, 137-56. List with biographical notes.

Ripple

BEARDMORE, H.L. 'A list of the rectors of Ripple', *A.C.* **27**, 1905, 237-54. See also **32**, 1917, 321-4.

MURIEL, EDWARD. 'Notes on Ruckinge church', *A.C.* **8**, 1872, 310-15. List of rectors, 1288-1870.

Rochester

YATES, NIGEL, ed. *Faith and fabric: a history of Rochester Cathedral, 604-1994.* Woodbridge: Boydell Press, 1996. Authoritative; includes list of priors and deans, 13-20th c.

Saltwood

ROBERTSON, W.A. SCOTT. 'Saltwood church', *A.C.* **18**, 1889, 421-32. Includes list of rectors, with biographical notes.

Seal

FRAMPTON, T. SHIPDEM. 'List of incumbents of St.Peter's, Seal (held with St. Mary's Kemsing, until 1874)', *A.C.* **20**, 1893, 258-75.

Seasalter

Seasalter communicants 1615-1710. Fiche. K.F.H.S.R.P. **1723**. 1996. Not seen.

Sheldwich

ROBERTSON, W.A. SCOTT. 'Sheldwich church', *A.C.* **18**, 1889, 288-303. Includes list of vicars, with biographical notes.

Shoreham Deanery

DUNCAN, LELAND L. 'Ecclesiological notes respecting the Deanery of Shoreham, Kent', *A.C.* **23**, 1898, 134-49. Primarily extracts from the wills of benefactors to churches.

Sibertswold

Shepherdswell & Coldred, Kent: composition and surplice fees, 1783-1820. 4 fiche. K.F.H.S.R.P. **345**. 1986. For 1821-51, see **346** (5 fiche). Filmed from the original manuscript.

Shepherdswell, Kent: offertory accounts, 1784-1867; briefs & collections 1731-1868, & cash bk. 3 fiche. K.F.H.S.R.P. **347**. 1986. Filmed from the original manuscripts.

Shepherdswell, Kent: offertory accounts 1902-11 & graveyard plan and PCC accts 1934-3. 2 fiche. K.F.H.S.R.P. **348**. 1986. Filmed from the original manuscripts.

Shepherdswell, Kent, Sunday School registers 1910-1923. 4 fiche. K.F.H.S.R.P. **340**. 1986. Filmed from the original registers.

Smallhythe

TAYLOR, A.H. 'The chapel of St. John the Baptist, Smallhythe', *A.C.* **30**, 1914, 133-91. Includes list of clergy, with biographical notes; also extracts from accounts, parish registers (of Tenterden), wills, *etc.*

TAYLOR, A.H. 'The clergy of St. John the Baptist, Smallhythe', *A.C.* **55**, 1943, 26-36. Includes brief notes.

Sturry

The confirmation register of Sturry, Kent, 1929-1956, and register of services 1959-1969. 5 fiche. K.F.H.S.R.P. **215**. [1986?] Filmed from the original manuscript.

Documents relating to the incumbent's property in Sturry, Kent. 2 fiche. K.F.H.S.R.P. **222**. [1968?] Filmed from the original manuscripts.

Induction, curates and marriage licences with some apprenticeship indentures & poor law papers. 2 fiche. K.F.H.S.R.P. **221**. [1986?] For Sturry. Filmed from the original manuscripts.

Register of persons confirmed or admitted to Holy Communion in the church of St. Nicholas, Sturry. 3 fiche. K.F.H.S.R.P. **214**. [1986?] Filmed from the original manuscripts. Covers 1868-75 and 1878-1927.

The register of services of Sturry, Kent, 1949-1959. 5 fiche. K.F.H.S.R.P. **216**. [1986?] Filmed from the original manuscript.

Sturry, Kent: church repairs and maintenance, 19th & 20th century; letters re church clock. 3 fiche. K.F.H.S.R.P. **269**. 1986. Filmed from the original manuscripts.

Tenterden

TAYLOR, A.H. 'The rectors and vicars of St. Mildred's, Tenterden, with an appendix', *A.C.* **31**, 1915, 207-74. Includes brief biographies. The appendix prints abstracts of various documents relating to ecclesiastical matters.

Thornham

CAVE-BROWNE, JOHN. 'The vicars of Thornham-cum-Aldington', *A.C.* **18**, 1889, 243-52. Includes biographical notes.

Tilmanstone

FRAMPTON, THOMAS SHIPDEM. 'List of forty-five vicars of Tilmanstone', *A.C.* **20**, 1893, 104-18.

Tonbridge Priory

FIELDING, C.H. 'Tonbridge Priory', *Invicta magazine* **2**, 1911, 76-85. Includes list of priors.

Trottescliffe

FRAMPTON, T.S. 'Fifty-eight rectors of Trottescliffe', *A.C.* **20**, 1893, 187-94.

Westbere

Westbere parish offertory accounts, 1888-1920. 4 fiche. K.F.H.S.R.P. **923**. [198-]. Filmed from the original accounts.

Westbere parish sacrament accounts, 1837-1846. 1 fiche. K.F.H.S.R.P. **922**. [198-]. Filmed from the original accounts.

Westbere Deanery

HUSSEY, ARTHUR. 'Visitations of the Archdeacon of Canterbury', *A.C.* **25**, 1902, 11-56; **26**, 1904, 17-50; **27**, 1905, 213-29; **28**, 1909, 75-82. Presentments of churchwardens in Westbere Deanery, 16-17th c.

Westenhanger

FRAMPTON, T. SHIPDEM. 'St. Mary's, Westenhanger (church destroyed): rectors and patron', *A.C.* **31**, 1915, 82-91. List with biographical notes, 13-17th c.

West Hythe

FRAMPTON, T. SHIPDEM. 'Vicars of St. Mary, Westhythe', *A.C.* **30**, 1914, 233-49. List with brief biographies.

Whitstable

BOWDEN, C., [ed.] *Whitstable: communicants 1637-1710; vestries 1712-1834; list of parish officers 1637-1725.* 2 fiche. K.F.H.S.R.P. **1639.** 1991.

Woodchurch

ROBERTSON, [W.A.] SCOTT. 'Woodchurch notes', *A.C.* **14,** 1882, 354-7. List of rectors, with biographical notes.

Wye

FRAMPTON, T.S. 'The vicars, masters or provosts, and perpetual curates, of the church of Ss. Gregory and Martin, Wye', *A.C.* **28,** 1909, 311-26.

B. Nonconformist Denominations

Publications on the history of Kentish nonconformity are fairly diffuse; there is no overall survey of use to genealogists. The works listed in section 14 of Raymond's *English genealogy: a bibliography* should, of course, be consulted. A history of the church in Kent, biased towards nonconformity, is supplied by:

TIMPSON, THOMAS. *Church history of Kent, from the earliest period to the year MDCCCLVIII, comprising I. Historical notices of Christianity in Kent from the earliest period to the Reformation. II. Memoirs of the Kentish protestant martyrs. III. Memorials of the Kentish non-conformist confessors. IV. Records of the independant churches in Kent.* Ward & Co., 1859. Includes 'biographies of the ministers ejected in Kent' in 1662.

Dissenting ministers who assented to the 39 articles of the Church of England are listed, with some biographical details, in:

RICKARD, GILLIAN, ed. *Kent dissenting ministers' declarations 1689-1836.* Canterbury: Gillian Rickard, 1995.

For records indexed at the Institute of Heraldic and Genealogical Studies in Canterbury, see:

HUMPHERY-SMITH, CECIL. 'Kent non-conformist records', *K.F.H.S.J.* 4(3), 1984, 99-101.

i. *Baptists*

BUFFARD, FRANK. *Kent and Sussex Baptist Associations.* Faversham: E.Vinson, 1963. Includes lists of moderators and officers since 1935.

CHAMBERS, RALPH FREDERICK. *The Strict Baptist chapels of England, volume III: Kent.* Thornton Heath: R.F. Chambers, 1955. Brief histories of particular churches

PAUL, S.F. *Further history of the Gospel Standard Baptists, vol. 5. Some Surrey and Kent churches.* Brighton: the author, 1966. Brief histories of particular churches.

Eythorne

Eythorne Baptist church records. 1 fiche. K.F.H.S.R.P. **1613.** 1990. Filmed from original manuscripts.

Eythorne Baptist Chapel minutes of church meetings, 1792-1843. 4 fiche. K.F.H.S.R.P. **1044.** 1989.

Eythorne Baptist Chapel minutes of deacons and church meetings 1839-1880. 4 fiche. K.F.H.S.R.P. **1045.** 1987.

Eythorne Baptist Chapel. Minutes of church meetings 1880-1924. 7 fiche. K.F.H.S.R.P. **1047.** 1987. Continued by:
  1049. 1924-1946. 2 fiche.
  1051. 1946-1973. 5 fiche.

Eythorn Baptist Chapel. Minutes of deacons meetings 1863-1903. 5 fiche. K.F.H.S.R.P. **1046.** 1989. Continued by:
  1048. 1904-1913. 5 fiche.
  1050. 1928-1946. 6 fiche.
  1052. 1946-1958. 5 fiche.
  1053. 1959-1965. Not seen.
  1054. 1965-1973. Not seen.

Eythorne Baptist Church, Kent: letters, testimonials, agreements, 19th century, with pastors, etc. 4 fiche. K.F.H.S.R.P. **1612.** 1990. Filmed from the originals.

Eythorne Baptist Church, Kent ... membership book: names with remarks e.g. 'died,' 'moved', etc., 1839 to 1900. 3 fiche. K.F.H.S.R.P. **1610.** 1990. Filmed from the original manuscript.

Eythorne Baptist Church, Kent: register of members, 1850s to 1946. Notes on how they were admitted, also notes on why they left. 5 fiche. K.F.H.S.R.P. **1611.** 1990. Filmed from the original manuscript.

. Congregationalists

Deptford
RCHENOUGH, JOSEPHINE. 'Barker's Chapel, Butt Lane, Deptford', *N.W.K.F.H.* **4**(3), 1986, 94-5. Brief notes on records of a Congregational chapel

Herne Bay
WATKINSON, J. *Herne Bay Congregational Church: history of the church with biographical notes of its ministers.* [Herne Bay?]: [ ], 1910.

Sheerness, etc.
GORDON, JOHN. *History of the Congregational churches of Sheerness, Queenborough, Minster, and the Isle of Grain, from the year 1725 to 1898.* 2nd ed. Sheerness: John Gordon, 1898. Includes some portraits of ministers.

ii. Huguenots
Huguenot records: a postscript', *Archives* **11**(52), 1974, 211-12. Summary of conference discussion, concerning records in Kent, Southampton, and Norfolk.

Canterbury
CROSS, FRANCIS W. *History of the Walloon & Huguenot church of Canterbury.* Publications of the Huguenot Society of London 15. 1898. Includes list of pastors, list of records, and many original documents. Extensive.

OAKLEY, ANNE M., ed. 'The Canterbury Walloon congregaion from Elizabeth I to Laud', in SCOULOUDI, IRENE, ed. *Huguenots in Britain and their French background 1550-1800.* Macmillan, 1987, 56-71. General study.

Dover
OVEREND, G.H. 'Strangers at Dover', *Proceedings of the Huguenot Society of London* **3**, 1888-91, 89-171 & 286-330. Includes lists of 'strangers', 1571 and 1622, various other 17th c. lists, and memoranda of baptism, marriages etc.

MINET, WILLIAM. 'The fourth foreign church at Dover, 1685-1731', *Proceedings of the Huguenot Society of London* **4**, 1891-3, 93-217. Includes many extracts from records including a list of names from the registers, and of those making 'reconnaisances', that is, applying for membership.

Faversham
TASSELL, J.S. 'Notes on the French Congregation at Faversham, Kent, and the part played by the families of Grueber and Pigou in the manufacture of gunpowder', *Proceedings of the Huguenot Society of London* **20**(1), 1959, 139-41. Includes pedigree of Grueber, 18th c.

'French congregation at Faversham in the late seventeenth century', *Proceedings of the Huguenot Society of London* **19**(6), 1959, 353-4. Includes brief register of Huguenot baptisms, 1696-1700.

Greenwich
MOORE, VERONICA. 'Greenwich and its Huguenot connections', *T.G.L.A.S.* **10**(2), 1986, 4-12. Includes extracts from registers, etc.

Sandwich
MOENS, W.J.C. 'The relief of the poor members of the French churches in England', *Proceedings of the Huguenot Society of London* **5**, 1894-6, 321-42. Appendix is a transcript of accounts from the Sandwich Walloon church, listing contributors to a poor fund, 1568.

iv. Jews

Canterbury
ADLER, MICHAEL. 'The Jews of Canterbury', *Jewish Historial Society of England transactions* **7**, 1912, 19-96. Includes many abstracts from medieval records.

'The Jews of medieval Canterbury', in ADLER, MICHAEL. *Jews of medieval England.* Edward Goldston, 1939, 49-124. Includes lists, 1160-1290; also extracts from various accounts.

Dover
WEBSTER, MARTYN C. 'The Jews of Dover and their records', *K.F.H.S.J.* **8**(4), 1996, 138-9.

The Jews of Dover and their records. Fiche. K.F.H.S.R.P. **1777**. 1996. Not seen.

v. Methodist

PITTS, HUBERT A. *XIX century fragments of Methodist history of Hythe, Sandgate, Dymchurch, Folkestone, Elham Valley and Sellindge.* [Hythe]: Hythe Methodist Church Trust, 1969. Includes lists of ministers.

CORPUS, GEOFFREY. 'On the circuit: Methodist records', *N.W.K.F.H.* **7**(2), 1995, 47-8. Notes on the records of the Rye Circuit at East Sussex Record Office; includes list of members of the Shoreham and Otford Society, 1775.

JUDD, WALTER D. *The record of Wesleyan Methodism in the Sevenoaks Circuit, 1746-1932* ... Bedford: Rush & Warwick (Bedford) Ltd., 1932.

vi. Quakers

DRAPER, GILLIAN. 'The first hundred years of Quakerism in Kent', *A.C.* **112**, 1994, 317-40. Includes table shewing 'trustees and purchasers of Quaker property in Cranbrook, 1658-1767'.

SHOWLER, KARL. *A review of the history of the Society of Friends in Kent, 1655-1966.* Canterbury: Canterbury Preparative Meeting of the Society of Friends, 1970. Includes list of Folkestone trustees, *etc.,* 17-20th c.

vii. Roman Catholics

Kent recusant history. [ ]: Kent Recusant History Society, 1979- . Important.

BELLENGER, DOMINIC. 'Some post Reformation Kent Benedictines', *Kent recusant history* **8-9**, 1982/3, 154-6. See also **10-11**, 1983/4, 194-6. Brief biographies.

CLIFTON, MICHAEL. 'Southwark Diocesan archives', *Catholic archives* **4**, 1984, 15-24. The modern Roman Catholic diocese covers five counties in S.E. England.

BUCKINGHAM, CHRISTOPHER. 'Catholic recusancy in Kent, 1559-1800', *Cantium* **1**, 1969, 1-14, 42-52 & 116-22. General outline.

RYAN, ANTHONY C.W. 'Extracts from the calendar of Quarter Sessions records, 1574-1622 concerning recusants', *Kent recusant history* **2**(1), 1992, 26-9. Lists names.

Blackheath Hundred

EGAN, MICHAEL. 'The Hundred of Blackheath: a handlist of Catholics', *Kent recusant history* **12-13**, 1984/5, 214-8.

EGAN, MICHAEL. 'To search after Catholics: the Hundred of Blackheath', *Kent recusant history* **8-9**, 1982/3, 162-3. List of Catholics presented by the constables, 1743.

Canterbury

COUSINS, DAVID. 'The Hales Place congregation in 1835', *Kent recusant history* **12-13**, 1984/5, 224-7. Lists the Canterbury congregation by street.

St. Thomas, Canterbury: Catholic confirmation registers, 1838-1900. 1 fiche. K.F.H.S.R.P. **431**. 1986. Filmed from the original registers.

2. EDUCATION

Educational records can provide much useful information to genealogists. School registers are particularly useful, and many may be found in the archives. For a listing of educational records, including many registers, see:

County Council education records. 15 fiche. K.F.H.S.R.P. **733-8.** 1986.

Three works provide names of Kent students in higher education:

PANTIN, W.A. *Canterbury College, Oxford.* Oxford Historical Society N.S., **6-8 & 30.** 1947-85. This College was dependant on Canterbury Cathedral Priory; these volumes include transcripts of accounts and various other documents, biographical notes on students, *etc.*

COCK, F.W. 'Kentish men at the University of Padua', *A.C.* **40,** 1928, 85-7. List, 1647-1778.

BOGGIS, R.J.E. *A history of St. Augustine's College, Canterbury.* Canterbury: Cross & Jackman, 1907. Includes a roll of wardens, sub-wardens, fellows, and past students of a college for training clergymen for colonial service.

There are a number of histories of individual schools, and a few school registers have also been published. School histories usually list headmasters; they may also contain the names of other teachers and/or pupils, and others connected with the school. The following list is not comprehensive; it includes only those works likely to be of genealogical value.

Blackheath

BIRCHENOUGH, JOSEPHINE. 'Some schools in West Kent', *N.W.K.F.H.* **6**(7), 1993, 223-4. Notes on the records of schools at Blackheath, Dartford, and Deptford.

KIRBY, JOHN WILLIAM. *The history of the Blackheath Proprietary School.* Blackheath: Blackheath Press, 1933. Extensive; includes 'The record of service in the Great War of the old boys of the school ...'.

MALIM, MARY CHARLOTTE, & ESCREET, HENRIETTA CAROLINE, eds. *The book of the Blackheath High School.* Blackheath School, 1927. Includes various list of staff and pupils.

Bromley

WHYLER, FRED. 'Bromley Charity School, 1716: subscribers', *N.W.K.F.H.* **1**(8), 1980, 229. List.

Canterbury

Clergy Orphan School
SIMMONDS, MARK JOHN. *Register of the Clergy Orphan School for Boys, 1751-1896.* Canterbury: St. Augustine's College, 1897. The school moved from Yorkshire, 1751-1804, to Acton, 1804-12, St. John's Wood, 1812-55, and to Canterbury, 1855-96. It took boys from throughout the country.

Kent College
Kent College, 1885-1935. Canterbury: Kent Country Newspapers, 1937. Includes 'register of old boys', and many other names associated with a Canterbury school.

Kings School
WOODRUFF, C.E. & CAPE, H.J. *Schola Regia Cantuariensis: a history of Canterbury School, commonly called the Kings School.* Mitchell Hughes & Clarke, 1908. Extensive; includes 'the school roll, 1808-1908'.

SIDEBOTHAM, J.S. *Memorials of the Kings School, Canterbury. Comprising brief notices of those therein educated ...* Canterbury: A. Ginder, et al, 1865.

Kings School, Canterbury, register, 1859 to 1931. Canterbury: Old Kings Scholars Association, 1932.

King's School, Canterbury: list of O.K.S. serving in His Majesty's forces, 1914-1915. Canterbury: Gibbs and Sons, 1915.

Catford
MORRIS, L.F. *A history of St. Dunstan's College.* [Catford]: St. Dunstans College, 1970. Includes various lists of names.

WATSON, NIGEL. *St. Dunstan's College: a centenary history 1888-1988.* Catford: St. Dunstan's Educational Foundation, 1989. Catford school; includes lists of courses and staff, *etc.*

COLLETT, D.W. *St. Dunstan's College Catford, London, S.E.6: roll of honour for the First World War, 1914-19.* The author, 1988.

Chartham

WELLER, MICHAEL J. '19th century school records', *Family tree magazine* 9(5), 1993, 44-5. Based on Chartham school log book.

Cheriton

GAVIN, ANITA. 'Parish account (probably around 1860/70): Cheriton National School buildings account', *K.C.* 6(3), 1991, 94-6. Lists subscribers.

Cranbrook

TARBUTT, WILLIAM. *An historical account of Dence's School and schoolmasters from 1568 to 1865, with some information respecting other public endowments under the will of William Dence.* Cranbrook: Derrett, 1866. Includes list of masters, 1568-1812.

Dartford

HUDSON, RONALD L. *History of Dartford Grammar School.* Dartford: Dimond & Co., 1966. Includes lists of staff (headmasters from 1605).

JENKINS, EDITH M. 'Some notes on the log book (1863-1894) of Dartford National Boys School', *Dartford Historical & Antiquarian Society newsletter* 8, 1971, 9-11. Brief description.

See also Blackheath

Denstone

GREENWOOD, E.T., ed. *The Denstone register 1873-1930.* Shrewsbury: Wilding & Son, 1932.

Deptford

See Blackheath

Detling

BROWN, JOAN G. 'Detling village school', *B.K.* 8(11), 1987, 677-82; 8(12), 1987, 741-7. Mentions many names 1856-1980.

Dover

Dover College register: centenary edition, October 1871-July 1971. Dover: Buckland Press, 1971.

EVANS, C.L. *Dover College register 1871-1924.* 4th ed. Dover: G.W. Grigg & Son, 1924.

Elham

The charity school accounts of Elham, & minutes, 1743-1800. 3 fiche. K.F.H.S.R.P. 289. 1986. For 1800-1909, see 290 (4 fiche Filmed from the original manuscript.

Correspondence and plans, Elham school, 1848-1950; Sir John William's Charity; church inventory, 1934. 9 fiche. K.F.H.S.R.P. 292. 1986. Filmed from the original manuscripts.

Faversham

MUNDEN, A.F. *Eight centuries of education in Faversham.* Faversham papers 9. Faversham: Faversham Society, 1972. Includes wills of two men named John Cole, 1532 and 1536, list of Grammar School masters, 1576-1972, licences grante to schoolmasters, 1581-1699, *etc.*

GIRAUD, FRANCIS F. *Extracts from wills and other documents relating to the objects and endowment of the Faversham district national schools.* Faversham: Faversham District National Schools. [1867

Greenwich

KIRKBY, J.W. 'Early Greenwich schools and schoolmasters', *T.G.L.A.S.* 3(5), 1930, 218-41. General history.

KIRKBY, JOHN WILLIAM. *History of the Roan School (the Greycoat School) and its founder.* Blackheath Press, 1929. At Greenwich; includes will of John Roan, 1644, and several lists of names.

'A register of the boys of the Roan School beginning November 1st 1705', *T.G.L.A.S.* 4(4), 1950, 173-82. Greenwich school register to 1712.

Lewisham

BEARDWOOD, H., ed. *The history of Colfe's Grammar School, 1652-1972.* 3rd ed. Christchurch: Christchurch Times, 1972. Includes various brief lists of names. Supersedes previous editions by Leland L. Duncan.

DUNCAN, LELAND L. *Colfe's Grammar School, Lewisham, and the Great War 1914-19, with rolls of honour and of service.* Worshipful Company of Leathersellers, 1929.

DUNCAN, LELAND L. 'A list of the head masters of Colfe's Grammar School, Lewisham from its foundation, 1652 to the present time', *Lewisham Antiquarian Society annual report* **9**, 1894, 1-14.

MORRIS, LESLIE FRANK. *A history of St. Dunstan's College.* [Lewisham]: The College, 1970. At Lewisham. Includes various lists of names.

Maidstone

PHILLIPS, G.B. *Maidstone Grammar School 1549-1965: a record.* Headley Bros., 1965. Includes list of headmasters, 1549-1941, and of scholarship and exhibition holders, 1924-1965.

STREATFIELD, FRANK. *An account of the Grammar School in the King's town and parish of Maidstone in Kent.* Oxford: Rogers and Broome, 1915. Includes various lists of names.

Ramsgate

BARNARD, HOWARD CLIVE, & TAYLOR, F.N. *Records (1909-1922) of the Ramsgate County School for Boys (now known as Chatham House School).* 2nd ed. Ramsgate: Chatham House, 1923. Includes the school register.

Register of St. Lawrence College, 1879 to 1953. 4th ed. 2 vols. [Ramsgate]: Old Lawrentian Society, 1955. v.1. 1879-1929. v.2. 1930-1953.

Rochester

The Roffensian register, containing the names of all members of the school from 1835 A.D. to 1936 A.D. 4th ed. Rochester: Mackays, 1937. Kings School, Rochester. Including staff and pupils.

Saint Nicholas at Wade

PARKER, RICHARD. *The schools of St. Nicholas-at-Wade, 1640-1957.* Canterbury: Gibbs and Sons, 1957. General study, with names.

Sandwich

CAVELL, JOHN, & KENNETT, BRIAN. *A history of Sir Roger Marwood's School, Sandwich, 1563-1963, with a life of the founder.* Sandwich: Cory Adams & Mackay for the Governors, 1963. Includes lists of staff, prefects, chairmen of governors, etc.

Sevenoaks

LENNOX, J.T. *Sevenoaks School and its founder, 1432-1932.* Sevenoaks: Caxton & Holmesdale Press, 1932. Includes lists of staff.

SCRAGG, BRIAN. *Sevenoaks School: a history.* Bath: Ashgrove Press, 1993. Extensive; includes list of headmasters, 15-20th c.

Sibertswold

Shepherdswell, Kent: school manager's minute book 1903-1948. 4 fiche. K.F.H.S.R.P. **339.** 1986. Filmed from the original minutes.

Sturry

Sturry, Kent: will Nich. Franklin, 1577; Copt Hall lease 1727: school vouchers 1855-7. 8 fiche. K.F.H.S.R.P. **262.** 1986. Filmed from the original manuscripts. Mainly relates to Sturry school.

Tenterden

TAYLOR, A.H. 'The Grammar Free School at Tenterden', *A.C.* **44**, 1932, 129-46. Includes notes on masters, 16-18th c.

Tonbridge

RIVINGTON, SEPTIMUS. *History of Tonbridge School, from its foundation in 1553 to the present date.* 4th ed. Rivingtons, 1925. Extensive.

HART, WALTER G. *The old school lists of Tonbridge School.* George Allen & Unwin, 1933. General discussion, followed by chapter on various different families.

HUGHES-HUGHES, W.O. *The register of Tonbridge School from 1820 to 1893, also list of exhibitioners &c., previous to 1820, and of head masters and second masters.* R. Bentley, 1893.

STEED, H.E., ed. *The register of Tonbridge School from 1826 to 1910; also lists of exhibitioners &c., previous to 1826, and of head masters and second masters.* 3rd ed. Rivingtons, 1911.

STEED, H.E., ed. *The register of Tonbridge School from 1847 to 1926 with a list of head masters and second masters from the foundation of the school.* Rivingtons, 1927.

FURLEY, H.D. *The register of Tonbridge School from 1861 to 1945, with a list of head masters and second masters from the foundation of the school.* Rivingtons, 1951. Supersedes previous editions.

KNOTT, C.H., ed. *The register of Tonbridge School, from 1900 to 1965, with a list of headmasters from the foundation of the school, and assistant masters from 1900.* [Tonbridge: The School], 1966.

COBB, T.C. *The register of Tonbridge School from 1920 to 1985, with a list of headmasters (from the foundation of the school) and assistant masters from 1920.* Tonbridge: Old Tonbridgian Society, 1986.

Tonbridge School and the Great War of 1914 to 1919: a record of the service of Tonbridgians ... Whitefriars Press, 1929.

13. MIGRATION

Our ancestors moved! Many of them emigrated to Australasia or North America; others immigrated from the continent. Many general works on this subject are listed in Raymonds *English genealogy: a bibliography*. The subject of migration from Kent in the nineteenth century will be dealt with in:

RICKARD, GILLIAN. *Emigration from Kent in the nineteenth century.* Canterbury: the author, forthcoming.

At present only a few brief articles and notes on emigration from Kent are available. For general discussion on 19th century emigration, see:

WELLER, MICHAEL. 'Far and away: emigration from Kent in the early nineteenth century'. *B.K.* **14**(12), 1993, 735-43; **15**(1), 1994, 39-41

Australia and New Zealand

BRADY, KEVIN R. 'Natives of Kent, who arrived in Sydney, Australia on board the 'Woodbridge' on September 15th, 1838, having left Portsmouth, England, on the 7th May 1838', *K.F.H.S.J.* **5**(6), 1988, 216.

HOAD, JOYCE. 'Were they discharged in New Zealand?' *N.W.K.F.H.* **6**(10), 1994, 322-4. Lists Kent soldiers discharged in New Zealand, mid-19th c.

KING, D.J. FRANCIS. 'From Staplehurst to Wellington: six pauper families from Staplehurst who emigrated to Wellington, New Zealand, in 1839', *A.C.* **109**, 1992, 181-9. Their surnames were Avery, Farmer, Hunt, Nash, Peckham, and Relf.

WOJCIECHOWSKA-KIBBLE, B. 'Assisted emigration from Kent, 1834-70', *J.K.L.H.* **10**, 1980, 7-8. Brief discussion of emigration to Australia and New Zealand.

'Britain-Australia bicentenary 1788-1988', *N.W.K.F.H.* **4**(9), 1988, 327-42. Collection of articles celebrating the bi-centenary; includes 1841 census listing of convicts awaiting transportation.

North America

PUTNAM, EBEN. *Two early passenger lists, 1635-1637.* Boston: New England Historic Genealogical Society, 1921. Reprinted from *New England historical and genealogical register* 1921. Lists passengers embarking at Sandwich. Includes biographical notes.

Dymchurch
'From Dymchurch parish: material expences of the emigrant to America, April 28 1832', *K.C.* 4(6), 1987, 156. Gives names.

Sandhurst
HULMES, NOREEN C. 'Emigration to the United States of America from Sandhurst, Kent, 1826, 1827, and 1828', *A.C.* 73, 1960, 235-43. Lists emigrants; based partly on parochial records.

Sandwich
PUTNAM, EBEN. 'Two early passenger lists', *New England historical and genealogical register* 76, 1921, 217-26. Lists emigrants, with their families and servants, who sailed from Sandwich, 1634 and 1637; includes biographical notes.

Tenterden
'Emigrants from the Tenterden district', *K.F.H.S.J.* 4(5), 1984, 177-8. Lists passengers to New York, 1828.

Woolwich
HOLMES, SUE. 'Wandering ancestors', *W.D.F.H.S.J.* 11, 1982, 8-10; 12, 1982, 17-19. List of emigrants from Woolwich to Canada on board H.M.S. Serapis, 1896.

Immigration
Kent is only a few miles from the Continent, and many aliens have settled in the county. Huguenots were particularly prominent, and reference should also be made to the works listed in section 11B above.

RICHARDSON, JOAN A. CAREW. 'To inhabit the realm peaceably and enjoy his goods', *N.W.K.F.H.* 7(1), 1995, 15-16. List of aliens who took an oath of fealty to Henry V, 1436.

AWTY, BRIAN G. 'Aliens in the ironworking areas of the Weald: the subsidy rolls 1524-1603', *Wealden iron: Bulletin of the Wealden Iron Research Group* 2nd series 4, 1984, 13-78. Extensive listing of aliens from the subsidy rolls.

ARLY, TRACEY. 'The immigrant experience', *History today* 36, 7/1986, 54-6. Discussion of the Huguenot refugees in 16th c. Canterbury.

MORANT, VALERIE. 'Stranger settlements in Maidstone', *Proceedings of the Huguenot Society of London* 19(5), 1957, 249-56. Includes subsidy return for 'strangers', i.e. aliens, 1585.

PETERS, JOHN. *A family from Flanders.* Collins, 1985. A study of various Huguenot families who settled in Kent, 16-17th c., especially Peters (De La Pierre) family.

Author Index

92

Martin, A. 54, 81
Martin, C. 75
Mate, M. 50
Matthews, M. 67
Maxwell, T. 29
Mayr-Harting, H. 11
Meaden, L. 43
Meates, G. 56
Melling, E. 10, 13, 22, 26, 33
Mercer, W. 41
Miller, G. 15, 29
Mills, D. 12
Mills, J. 17
Mills, M. 49
Milton, H. 27
Minet, W. 85
Moens, W. 85
Mommsen, W. 11
Monson, L. 28, 59
Montmorency, J. 21
Moody, R. 32
Moore, D. 27
Moore, J. 12
Moore, R. 11
Moore, V. 85
Morant, V. 91
Morgan, P. 39
Morley, M. 33
Morris, L. 87, 89
Morris, P. 54
Mortimer, R. 48
Moylan, P. 13
Muggeridge, S. 30
Muhlfeld, H. 54
Munden, A. 88
Murfin, L. 16
Muriel, E. 82
Murphy, M. 46
Murray, K. 70
Muskett, P. 31
Myhil, O. 46

Neame, A. 70, 71
Neilson, N. 49, 51
Newman, A. 13, 62
Newman, J. 10
Nichol, R. 45
Nicholas, F. 50
Nichols, J. 9
Nicol, R. 29
Nield, B. 27

Norman, P. 27
Norman, W. 58
Norwood, J. 47
Norwood, P. 45
Nunn, F. 21
Nunns, G. 53, 65

O'Day, R. 49
O'Hara, D. 11
Oakley, A. 85
Oakley, M. 64
Oliver, D. 55
Oosterveen, K. 13
Orridge, B. 59
Orwin, C. 18
Osborn, T. 27
Oswald, A. 54
Outhwaite, R. 12
Overend, G. 85
Owen, D. 20
Owen, K. 25
Oyler, T. 74

Packer, J. 28
Pantin, W. 87
Panton, F. 64, 73
Parker, R. 89
Parker, S. 77
Parkin, E. 54, 56
Parking, E. 78
Parry, C. 43
Paul, S. 84
Pearce, K. 31
Pearman, A. 13, 54, 77, 78
Penney, C. 44
Perkyns, A. 16, 17
Peters, J. 91
Peters, K. 23
Petley-Jones, D. 59, 63
Philipot, J. 61
Phillips, G. 89
Phippen, J. 37
Pinhorn, M. 55
Pitts, H. 86
Plomer, H. 63
Pocknell, E. 28
Poland, J. 29
Pollard, T. 11
Ponsonby, C. 33
Poole, E. 23, 38, 59
Poos, L. 77
Porteus, G. 64

Post, J. 73
Poste, B. 81
Powell, W. 50
Pragnell, H. 80
Proudfoot, W. 57
Putnam, B. 60
Putnam, E. 90, 91

Ramsay, N. 78
Rawling, J. 33
Rawson, M. 41
Reay, B. 12-16
Reilly, L. 20, 21
Rhind, N. 27, 54
Rhodes, A. 59
Rhodes, N. 33
Richardson, J. 91
Rickard, G. 30, 33, 42, 61, 84, 90
Riddell, B. 23, 34
Riley, H. 51, 66, 68-70, 72
Rivington, S. 89
Roake, M. 10
Robertson, W. 23, 31, 48, 55, 56, 74, 76, 78, 80-82, 84
Robinson, T. 47
Roome, K. 15, 30
Rothstein, N. 31
Ruderman, A. 13, 43
Russell, J. 16
Russell, R. 33
Rutton, W. 31
Ryan, A. 86

Salisbury, E. 69
Salter, H. 51
Sandys, C. 47
Sattin, D. 26
Saunders, D. 25, 27
Saw, R. 51
Saxby, J. 56
Sayers, J. 49
Saynor, J. 71
Scally, M. 65
Scargill-Bird, S. 52
Scarisbrick, J. 29
Schofield, R. 13
Schuler, S. 11
Scott, J. 31, 51
Scouloudi, I. 85
Scragg, B. 89

Family Name Index

Place Name Index

100